GUINEA'S MINES UNVEILED

Facts, challenges and prospects

Abdoulaye MAGASSOUBA

GUINEA'S MINES UNVEILED

Facts, challenges and prospects

L'Harmattan

5-7, rue de l'Ecole-Polytechnique, 75005 Paris

http://www.editions-harmattan.fr

ISBN : 978-2-336-43257-1
EAN : 9782336432571

Contents

Acknowledgements

I dedicate this book to my late father, Mamady, who did everything to give me the best legacy there is: education and training. May his soul rest in peace!

I also extend a big thank you to everyone without whom this book would not have come to life:

To my wife, my children, and my parents, for their continuous support and affection.

To my friends for their unwavering support in the most difficult times, and assistance in the writing of this book.

To my collaborators in the Ministry of Mines, some of whom have contributed in one way or another to the drafting of certain parts of this book, and who are the principal actors in all the substance of this work. Without their work, there would have been no material to write this book.

To former Prime Ministers, Mamady Youla and Ibrahima Kassory Fofana and, to my colleagues with whom I have constantly worked for the implementation of the actions covered by this book.

Finally, to the Head of State under whose mandate I served, Professor Alpha Condé, without whom the subject of this book would have been, at best, only a dream.

Introduction

I was informed, on this Friday afternoon, March 13, 2020, that the Head of State would declare in the evening a state of health emergency due to the Covid-19 epidemic. I found myself praying that this news spare us the horrors of the Ebola epidemic. The years 2014 and 2015 were horrific for the country in terms of loss of life and economic loss. Very quickly, I started making calls to mining company executives to assess the situation. I was first surprised, then relieved by their composure. First, I attributed this to the positive outlook for the control of the pandemic by China, the main destination of production and source of financing for the Guinean mining industry. Then, I realized that the serenity, and especially the fighting spirit of the Guinean mining actors, is no mere coincidence. The year 2020 was vastly different from 2014.

From now on, it was not a question, for most players, to decide whether to invest. It is a question of doing everything not to halt the operations whose launching required, for several of them, hundreds of millions of dollars of investments. The new dynamic in the sector, for several years, has made quite a difference. It was no longer a question of making every effort to convince the miners to stay. We needed to focus more on supporting and accompanying them in this difficult time. Therefore, without delay we took measures to limit the health, commercial and financial risks to which mining activities were exposed; at best, we organized ourselves internally to be more efficient on the essential while preparing for the end of the crisis. Admittedly, we have had our share of crises and handling this one was not insuperable; even if it is of a different nature and dimension, with global repercussions.

For a country endowed with unparalleled potential, but as poor as Guinea, despite the progress made thanks to the profound reforms undertaken from 2011, the challenge was enormous when I took office as Minister of Mines. Especially when one is aware of the famous theory of the natural resource curse. However, my optimistic attitude has always been that, in our case, it was not a resource curse, but a simple paradox that needed to be corrected. Guinea is a resource-rich country, with enormous potential in agriculture, hydroelectricity and of course, for mining. We are home to the largest untapped deposit of high-grade iron ore in the world. Yet, we hardly ever produced a single tonne of it. We have therefore not exploited our resources enough to be in a situation of irreversible curse.

During my first days in office, I noticed that important and far-reaching reforms had been initiated. In the months that followed, I found myself dreaming of the impossible. Over the years, I have been part of an exhilarating journey, even though the most beautiful chapters of the story are yet to be written.

The paradox is about to fade, giving way to the story of a proud country that is moving towards fullness in the realization of its mining potential. However, as in a marathon, the last kilometers will be the most difficult. These last kilometers that must be managed much better than the first to avoid losing all the efforts already made. Especially since the expectations are enormous, even disproportionate, while the impact is gradual. Misunderstandings live up to expectations. Confusion too.

Feeling the responsibility to share my observations, hopes and fears, analyzes, and experiences, I decided to write.

I decided to write to bear witness to what has been accomplished to make progress in a sector that has long languished, the challenges faced, the lessons learned from my experience as minister of mines, and the prospects. To also emphasize that the journey ahead is still a long one, that an almost sacred, non-partisan union is needed around mining, to see it through, not only for our own sake but especially for future generations.

I also decided to write to prevent some, for lack of accurate information on this complex industry, from saying one day that they did not play their part because they " did not know ", so that everyone could assume their responsibilities at an important turning point in the development of Guinea's mines.

This book is intended for professionals and students aspiring to practice in the public and private fields. They are entitled to our side of the story, to explanations and analyzes of what mining development is precisely in the Guinean context, as part of a new mining policy. It is also intended for the average citizen who must be informed with a certain pedagogy to be conversant with mining and fully play his role, discern the true from the false, make the difference between the rantings and ravings and the complex realities of an industry that stretches its tentacles across the economy and involves more than ten departments and agencies daily. Investors must also have access to information and analyzes from stakeholders on the reforms undertaken in the sector, on the vision that underpinned these reforms and on the conditions for implementing actions intended to improve the investment framework.

This book therefore has an educational and clarification objective so that everyone can form an opinion on the development of mining with full knowledge of the facts. Also, without claiming to express the positions of the Guinean State, it serves to honor the duty of accountability through the transparency established in the management of the sector.

In this book, you will find explanations on the reality of the implementation of a reform agenda in Guinea's mines, some major facts and anecdotes presented with the necessary precautions, but also and above all the lessons and analyzes of an experience. You may have a different opinion than mine. But you will have a reasoned and explained opinion from me.

I have endeavored to explain at times what may seem simple to industry experts because this work is intended for a wide audience. I implore the indulgence of experts in advance. Also, the substance of this book was finalized in December 2020 (while I was in office). The facts and analyses included therein are therefore prior to 2021 and mainly cover the period 2016-2020. They may not necessarily take into account subsequent developments, except for a few prospective analyses to be treated with caution. The numerical data mentioned in this book come from official statistics published or produced upon request by the Ministry of Mines unless indicated otherwise.

Before getting to the heart of the matter, I would like to share what has represented for me, in addition to the new mining policy formalized in the 2011 Mining Code (amended in 2013)[1], the compass of our actions, the

---

1 https://mines.gov.gn/wp-content/uploads/2023/08/Code_Minier_2011_amende_2013_bilingue_FR-EN.pdf

roadmap for the first five years I spent at the head of the Ministry of Mines: my inaugural speech, which outlines the principles of governance and my intentions for the position of Minister of Mines that I was about to assume.

Conakry, January 7, 2016

I am today filled with a deep sense of humility in the face of the heavy responsibility that the President of the Republic, President Alpha Condé, and the Prime Minister, Head of Government, Mr. Mamady Youla, have honored me with. I would like to thank them and assure them of my firm commitment to honor this trust through every action I will take in this ministry for the effective development of our mines, so that it can fully play its role as a catalyst for the development of our country.

Ladies and gentlemen,

The path we are about to embark on together, with all stakeholders in this sector, for the benefit of all, will not be easy, but the common interest that will guide our actions will certainly energize us towards achieving the goal of accelerated development in this industry. Everyone should benefit from it. Investors must be treated with the utmost respect so that hopes can be transformed into projects that create viable employment for our people and wealth for partners and the entire nation. This is only possible in an investment-friendly environment and within a framework of mutually beneficial partnerships. Attracting investments to the sector is the key to this prosperity.

Dear Mining Workers,

To attract investments in a globally competitive framework among countries, we need public players to deliver a quality service exclusively motivated by the common interest. To fully leverage current and future opportunities, it is necessary to establish robust and coordinated government policies that will foster the growth of the sector, which is the linchpin for facilitating the economic diversification of our country. Emphasis will be placed on good governance, transparency, and performance.

The responsibility of everyone is engaged in the success of the reform of the mining industry. For our part, our primary responsibility is to create the necessary working conditions for delivering this exemplary public service. We also bear the responsibility of fair and equitable treatment of the workers in this department.

Everyone will be judged by their actions, by their results. The effectiveness of your actions will be appreciated through the substantial improvement of the sector's contribution to the transformation of the Guinean economy in line with the vision of the President of the Republic. The quality of this contribution, from which all Guineans will benefit, including each one of us, will primarily depend on the rigor, creativity, and patriotism that you put into each of your actions. I count on you so that each one can be an example that inspires beyond the mines. I will invest all my strength, all my determination, to achieve this result with you.

Honorable guests,

Much has been accomplished by my predecessor, the Minister of State, Dr. Kerfalla Yansané, who spared no time and energy to continually lay the foundations for the development of the sector. We thank him for the work he has done. I had the privilege of witnessing this effort from the forefront. Now, we must dedicate ourselves to completing the initiated reforms and accelerating the development of the mines.

To succeed in the reform agenda, we need responsible mining companies committed to the diligent implementation of their projects, adhering to the current regulations, and behaving as development actors, in addition to their legitimate goal of satisfying their shareholders. We need genuine corporate citizens, recognizing the shared responsibility they bear in the success of the development of our mines and, beyond that, our economy.

We will ensure, on our part, that the State fully takes its responsibilities to guarantee that all stakeholders honor their respective commitments and, more broadly, to continue efforts to improve the investment climate in Guinea.

Honorable guests,

The mining sector, more than any other, is exposed to the uncertainties of the global economic and financial environment, challenges that the mining administration cannot ignore. By listening to each other, each of us must inevitably understand the challenges brought about by the vicissitudes of international markets.

For Guinea, the only way to avoid continually bearing the brunt of these market shocks is to anticipate them, create more resilience, and strengthen our presence. That's why, beyond accelerating ongoing projects, our goal will also be to diversify the exploited mining resources and facilitate the creation and development of new projects. We must seize opportunities in a timely manner so as not to remain perpetual observers of markets where our unique potential, in Africa and globally, predisposes us to become a key leader. We must, therefore, take control of our destiny to ensure the sector's effective impact on the development of our country.

Beyond revenue for the state and communities, the true impact of mining inevitably lies in the creation of local expertise in terms of workforce and Guinean SMEs, with the objective not only of creating multiplier effects in other sectors but also establishing Guinea as an exporter of expertise in Africa and beyond. A qualified local workforce and competitiveness in other factors of production will also attract more investment to the country. While keeping in mind legitimate constraints of supply and schedule, I will strongly encourage all mining companies to adopt a proactive approach in promoting local capacities, which are often more cost-effective.

These local capacities and the development of the energy sector will also be the viable foundation for the local transformation of our raw materials. We must, with private partners, in our common interest, continue to work towards the local transformation of our ores.

Dear partners,

Dear members of professional organizations and civil society,

Dear colleagues and collaborators,

We must all work together to achieve a shared and embraced vision of the role of the mines in the development of Guinea to derive the best benefits for all stakeholders. This is the mission that the President of the Republic has entrusted to me. Everything will be done to ensure better harmony, better dialogue, and a better balance of relationships in partnerships among all stakeholders. Because the health of our partnerships is the key to success. The stability and sustainability of our relationships rely on a genuine balance of interests, as a partnership that is not balanced is inherently unstable in the long run.

Let us work together because we can only succeed together.

By working in harmony, with mutual trust, we can irreversibly set Guinea on the path of transforming the promise that our mines have always held into a reality of jobs and prosperity for the Guinean people and our partners.

It is good to be recognized for one's potential, but it is even better to be recognized for one's prosperity.

Long live Guinea.

Thank you.

1

At the core of priority projects

Here I am at a crossroads. After many years of working in the private sector; after several months of preparation and consultation on my planned role within the Presidency of the Republic, I am impatient. An unjustified impatience since I am already put to work. I attended my first official meeting at the Ministry of Mines at the very beginning of this month of February 2013. A meeting on the Simandou iron ore project. Like an omen. A bit impertinent, I expressed my fears there vis-à-vis these legal advisers who seemed to be directing the debates rather than advising the government. I am already concerned about the ineffectiveness and risk of such an approach in the new mining policy. I attempted to embrace this role of a form of efficiency facilitator assigned to me on priority issues.

Since his election in 2010, the Head of State has called upon expertise from various backgrounds to make his governance as effective as possible and minimize bureaucracy in the administration. Among other initiatives, he sought the support of the Africa Governance

Initiative (AGI[2]), Tony Blair's Initiative for Governance in Africa.

After his tenure as British Prime Minister (1997-2007), Mr. Blair created this organization to provide support to States in the context of improving governance. In Guinea, the support of this entity in the organization of the administration of the presidency and the monitoring of priority projects seemed useful. However, the President of the Republic wanted to go further by drawing inspiration from one of the main successes of Mr. Blair's governance during his time as Prime Minister: the Delivery Unit. This agency was responsible, based on specific priorities and indicators, for ensuring that the Prime Minister's objectives were effectively achieved in the priority areas. The President was rightly inspired by this model, which has been adopted in different forms by several other countries.

I had already been providing my support free of charge to certain administrations, including the cabinet of the presidency, for a few months, when it was proposed to me to reflect on the design and implementation of an adapted version of this agency within the presidency. This mission was entrusted to me after several opportunities to enter the administration which had not materialized for various reasons. I had already declined certain offers that were made to me within the ministries because they did not seem sufficiently interesting to me to have the desired impact. These offers were the result of steps voluntarily taken by the former Prime Minister, François Lonseny FALL, who took me under his wings in 2009 by appointing me secretary in charge of economic affairs for his brand-new political party, the United Front for

[2] AGI was established in 2008 to "support leaders in Presidencies and Ministries across Africa to help them turn their visions for development into reality through effective government".

Democracy and Change (FUDEC). After merging his party into the presidential party, the Rally of the People of Guinea – Rainbow (RPG Arc-en-ciel), he continued his efforts to appoint young executives, including myself, in whom he spotted potentials for a strong contribution to public action. His efforts, for which I can only be grateful, and those of advisers to the Head of State, finally enabled the latter to discover me and entrust me with setting up this "Delivery Unit".

From August 2012, I devoted a good part of my time to this mission of setting up what would later become the Monitoring and Support Office of the Presidency (BSAP). I had a unique opportunity to support the country's priority projects. There could not be a better introduction to help advance the national development agenda. I first drafted and submitted the strategy adapted to the Guinean context, as well as a proposal on the appropriate organization and functioning for the BSAP. After all my consultations and readings on the subject, including the reference in the matter of Michael Barber ("*Instruction to Deliver*")[3]. The preparation process, which I hoped would be short, finally lasted more than six months.

The Monitoring and Support Office of the Presidency (BSAP) was finally created on February 8, 2013. My appointment followed, a few weeks later, on March 5, 2013. A new phase, laden with uncertainties and hopes, fears and dreams, was unfolding in my career. The transition that I had started in 2006 towards the public administration was coming to an end. Six years of meticulous preparation had made it possible to reach this new starting point. I was prepared for the sacrifices that the public administration demanded from a private sector intruder, with its prejudices of arrogance and smugness

---

[3] Michael Barber, Instruction to Deliver: Fighting to Transform Britain's Public Services, Methuen Publishing Ltd, May 2008

towards the public administration. This long preparation allowed me to accept without flinching the small vestibule in a satellite building of the Presidency of the Republic, commonly called "The Little Palace ", which served as my office for long weeks before I was assigned a more decent office on the 4th floor of that same building. A safe my size, a remnant of another time, dominated this cramped, windowless space. Once installed, it took more than six months for me to receive my first monthly salary from the State, and a few more to finally have my official vehicle. Despite this situation, which made me spend a good part of my savings during my first year, I was hardly bored. Above all, I flourished with an indescribable pleasure in working on subjects as important for the country as those of mining, energy, and agriculture.

My first official meeting, held at the Ministry of Mines, was indeed an omen. For long months, I was going to spend long days, on the Simandou project[4], during my three years in this position. In line with BSAP concept a structure of support and not of execution, I pleaded not to be around the negotiation tables, not to be in the execution, but rather to support the teams who intervened. Our needs in operational capacities and my personal involvement very quickly made evident the need for a participation beyond my expectations. I was chosen, along with adviser Idrissa Thiam, to join the working group set up following the meeting of the Head of State with the management of Rio Tinto on the sidelines of the Abu Dhabi forum, in November 2013. Mr. Thiam, a brilliant mind like you rarely meet in life, took me into confidence

[4] The blocks 3 and 4 of Simandou mine developed by Simfer S.A, which is owned by the Government of Guinea (15%) and Simfer Jersey Limited (85%). Simfer Jersey Limited is a joint venture between the Rio Tinto Group (53%) and Chalco Iron Ore Holdings (47%).

and gave me all the space I needed to express myself professionally. It was also an opportunity to get to know Dr Alkaly Yamoussa Bangoura, the President's adviser in charge of mining issues who, instead of seeing my presence on this very important mining project as a threat to his space, opened up to me with great generosity and introduced me to complex mining issues. With other executives from the Ministries of Mines, Finance and Budget, we formed a team for nearly two years with which I learned a lot. My collaboration with these competent executives within the Simandou South Working Group reinforced my conviction of the existence of unsuspected resources within the public administration. This conviction had emerged during my interactions with the Ministry of Health in the mid-2000s.The intrinsic good quality of these senior civil servants, who did their basic university studies in Guinea, revealed to me that of education under the first regime[5] (from 1958 to 1984).

In addition to the technical learning of the mining industry within the Working Group, this experience, over the months, provided me with a better understanding of the intricacies of administration. The negotiation missions, which became increasingly frequent, were an opportunity for me to spend long hours discussing with team members and learning from them. The lawyers and other advisors also provided me with a perspective more in line with the realities and complexities of the global mining industry, beyond the nationalist perspective that we tended to have. At the end of these negotiations, I had crossed a threshold; I had matured several years in one.

Alongside the mines, the energy field has been a focal point of my responsibilities from the very beginning. In July 2013, I was appointed as the rapporteur of the

[5] The first regime, led by President Ahmed Sékou Touré, ruled Guinea from its independence in 1958 until the President's death in 1984.

permanent inter-ministerial committee for monitoring and steering the energy field, established to assess the state of the sector and propose measures to improve electricity supply, which was far from the desired level despite the substantial investments made by the state.

In this commission, composed of several ministers under the chairmanship of the Minister of Economy and Finance, Kerfalla Yansané, I came to understand the depth of the challenges in this sector. Between the issues of losses and the management of the national company, Électricité De Guinée (EDG), and the lack of investment in energy projects for over a decade, the challenge was enormous. Despite the efforts of the new CEO, Mr. Nava Touré, in an environment that was not always favorable, the task was truly colossal. Even the establishment of the EDG oversight committee did not effectively address this challenge in the short term.

My initial working relationship with the Minister of Economy and Finance began within the energy monitoring committee. A former Governor of the Central Bank of the Republic of Guinea (BCRG) for many years and a future Minister of Mines, the name Kerfalla Yansané is inseparable from the recent history—or indeed, the entire history—of our country. His experience and legendary composure piqued my curiosity and admiration. We began to interact during the early sessions of the committee, during which I did not limit myself to simply taking notes in my role as rapporteur. Very quickly, he began seeking my opinion on subjects sometimes unrelated to the committee's work. I immediately seized this opportunity to open up to a relationship that could only help me grow through the absorption of his invaluable experience. Every trip abroad in his company was an opportunity for me to learn from his long and captivating history. I remember that, by bombarding him with questions, there were times when our fellow travelers had to remind us not to miss a connecting flight during a layover. As always, I had a thirst for the experiences of others to build and enrich my own. I hope that he will one day write his memoirs, as many others who have the legitimacy and responsibility to do so.

In the field of energy, another major project was Souapiti, the largest dam in the country located on the Konkouré River. I was tasked with revising the initial memorandum of understanding for this project with the future builders, CWE (a subsidiary of China Three Gorges Corporation[6]). With the support of lawyers and through lengthy but ultimately productive negotiations with CWE's representatives, we established a balanced general framework that would later serve as the basis for negotiating agreements, despite a few twists and turns. My first meeting with the builders was one of these episodes.

Sitting in my office one Saturday morning, I received a call from the officials of CWE whom I had never met before. I agreed to meet them without really knowing exactly what they were going to ask for. For me, it was still an opportunity to improve the proposal that had been submitted for review. I found the three men in question to be cheerful, open, and very enthusiastic. A cordial and lively discussion followed, with demonstrations of commercial and financial schemes that could rival a project management course. To my surprise, my interlocutors agreed on almost all the ten points I wanted to renegotiate. This initial step led to the signing of the memorandum of understanding on September 29, 2015, the day after the launch of the Kaléta dam's operation

[6] China Three Gorges Corporation (CTG) is a Chinese state-owned enterprise that was founded in 1993, built the world's largest power station in terms of installed capacity (22,500 MW) from 1994 to 2012 across the Yangtze River.

(downstream from Souapiti on the Konkouré River[7]). Souapiti was a major energy project for the second term in which the Head of State would be a candidate a few weeks later. A negotiation commission was immediately established, led by El Hadj Nassirou Diallo, an advisor to the Head of State in charge of energy, under the supervision of the presidential economic team led by Ibrahima Kassory Fofana (future Prime Minister). I had a fruitful and enlightening collaboration with El Hadj Nassirou Diallo, a man with a strong character skillfully hidden by a certain discretion, notable integrity, intellectual honesty, and wisdom.

These preliminary negotiations also benefited from the insights and leadership of Minister of State Ibrahima Kassory Fofana. His contribution was critical in the negotiation process for the project, which required a familiarity with public-private partnerships that few others in the administration possessed. This "elder brother," known for his strong yet approachable character, surrounded me with affection and offered regular guidance. He had previously served as the Minister of Finance after many years in roles related to investment management and the agency in charge of major projects.

We spent most of the year 2015 in this negotiation process. Two major points of concern revolved around the project's cost and local content. We were convinced, or at least had a strong feeling, that the project was too expensive. So, we requested the international consulting firm hired for this purpose to provide us with a comparative evaluation. The firm's findings were quite

[7] The Konkouré River arises in west-central Guinea and flows into the Atlantic Ocean. Garafiri (75 MW of installed capacity), Souapiti (450 MW), Kaléta (240 MW) and Amaria (300 MW, under development) are the dams on the river to provide the country with much of its electricity.

enlightening. The Souapiti dam would cost around 3 million US dollars per installed megawatt. However, Souapiti was only half as expensive as Garafiri (nearly 6 million US dollars per installed megawatt), one of the most expensive dams in the reference sample. The cost per installed megawatt at Kaléta remained the most attractive, as the facility benefits from a natural drop in elevation and reduced environmental costs compared to Souapiti, according to the consulting firm. Souapiti was, to some extent, disadvantaged by natural conditions and the size of the population to be resettled. The conclusion was that the cost of developing Souapiti was above the median of the projects in the reference sample. However, many projects in the reference sample had a higher cost per installed megawatt, not to mention the increase in annual energy production at Kaléta due to the water reservoir from Souapiti. Despite some reassurance from these findings, we still wanted to attempt negotiations to reduce the project's cost. So, we initiated discussions on this front.

In parallel, for several months, the World Bank had initiated a study on the project, with the primary goal of determining its estimated cost. We were in the midst of tense negotiations. Aiming for a reduction between 5% and 10%, we had scheduled a session that we hoped would be decisive when the announcement of the World Bank's findings was made at a local hotel. Naturally, all parties decided to attend this presentation before continuing the negotiations. We were disappointed to discover during this meeting that the cost estimated by the World Bank exceeded the one proposed by CWE! We were disappointed with the result, not with the quality of the work, which could be considered independent and rigorous. The study conducted by reputable professionals was not commissioned by any of the parties for the purpose of negotiation.

The meeting that followed with CWE was brief. We had to face the facts: the cost presented by CWE was acceptable, and we had no room for maneuver. So, we focused our efforts on other equally important aspects, such as the portion of purchases that the company was required to make in the local Guinean market. CWE's representatives wanted tax benefits and began approaching the commission for this purpose. Personally, I had no issue with an important public project like this one benefiting from tax incentives. However, in return, the company had to commit to purchasing locally anything it could find at a competitive cost and under the expected quality conditions. That is how I responded when they shared their intention to request tax exemptions with me. I then advocated this position within the commission.

The primary target of local sourcing was cement, which was to be used in significant quantities for the dam's construction. The company's officials took on this challenge and initiated negotiations with local cement producers. The efforts made by some local cement manufacturers to meet the requirements in terms of quantity, quality, and timing led to new investments and job creation. These industries supplied more than 400,000 tonnes of cement for the construction of Souapiti. Some expanded their operations and sustained their businesses, subsequently benefiting from increased demand from the mining industry. These positive impacts and other collateral effects added to the main objective of the negotiations on the dam construction contract, which was energy production.

After my departure from the presidency, I followed from a distance the negotiation and signing of this contract in January 2016. Based on this, CWE immediately initiated the project using its own funds, without waiting for the negotiation and signing of the financing agreement (which included partnership structuring and financing terms). This agreement was only concluded in September 2018. From the outset, we had demanded and secured the hiring of internationally renowned legal, technical, and financial advisors to assist the state in this complex arrangement within the framework of a public-private partnership.

In addition to the specific issues related to the mining, energy, and agriculture fields, the Presidential Monitoring and Support Office (BSAP) was also involved in tracking government actions. My initial months at the presidency coincided with the establishment of "sectoral meetings." These meetings brought together ministers from specific sectors and their collaborators. Groupings were made by domain, such as rural development (agriculture, livestock, and fisheries), economic domains, educational domains, etc. On one side, these ministries presented the state of their field and sometimes the management of specific issues. On the other side, the Head of State, surrounded by his advisors, including myself, asked questions and gave instructions. The presence of the ministers' collaborators made the format of this forum unusual. Moreover, in an atmosphere of free speech, it was not surprising that some officials took advantage of the presence of the highest authority in the country to try to make themselves stand out or settle scores with their ministers. It could happen that an ambitious collaborator of a minister would go so far as to strongly contradict them during a session or, in rare cases, raise their voice against the minister! While the opportunistic behavior of some officials did not surprise me, the "courage" with which some dared to present inaccurate information to the country's chief executive was astonishing.

For my part, these meetings allowed me to become familiar with the key socioeconomic sectors of the country. In just a few days, we could move from the annual agricultural campaign to diagnosing EDG, while also discussing public procurement. Even more importantly, these meetings provided an opportunity for my initial regular interactions with the Head of State.

I also noticed that the President's blunt reactions and perplexing questions easily intimidated his interlocutors, particularly when they had personal interests to defend instead of the public interest, or when their arguments were weak, inconsistent, and lacking in facts. There was no room for error. As was his habit, he systematically read all documents. With an exceptional memory, he often reminded certain interlocutors of what they had written or even said just a few weeks earlier.

Observing these interactions greatly assisted me in the years that followed. I made it a point to always have a strong and objective foundation for defending the positions I proposed, ensuring that only the country's best interests justified these positions. I dare to believe that the Head of State increasingly appreciated our interactions during these sectoral meetings and during trips to promote investments, paying more attention to the advice I provided. The price was constant availability day and night to meet the expectations of this workaholic who could call at 11 p.m. or 6 a.m. to inquire about the progress of a file or simply to ask questions and push you to your limits on a subject. Days with him were long and intense, both in Guinea and especially abroad. Those who did not interact with him on a daily basis were surprised when they hear about this hyperactivity. His half-century struggle reflected his passion, which I would describe as a visceral commitment to Guinea's development. However, not everyone could withstand the intensity, energy, and impatience for results that can exhaust even the toughest of his collaborators.

Over the months, while working on the priority issues in mining, energy, and agriculture, my involvement expanded to include relations with international investors as I participated in the President's trips and meetings. This allowed me to better understand the perception and motivations of investors and other partners who had long been affected by a disappointing, and even traumatizing experience for some. An experience that had kept them away from the country, despite our enormous agricultural, mining, and tourism potential, among others. After 2010, it took several years of tireless efforts to see a positive shift in this perception. Changing a bad reputation is a long and frustrating journey for those involved, who hope for a dramatic leap but often experience only gradual progress. The three years I spent in the presidency helped me understand just how long and challenging the road was toward creating a business environment that instills total confidence in Guinea among serious investors.

To effectively respond to the President's increasingly frequent and appreciated requests, I received valuable guidance and advice within the presidency. The support of Naby Youssouf Bangoura, Minister Secretary-General of the Presidency, was extremely helpful during this period. Kiridi, as he is commonly known, held high positions in the administration in his thirties, eventually becoming the Minister of Territorial Administration. His career inspired me to the extent that during our first meeting, I detained him in the stairwell of the "small palace" for several hours while bombarding him with questions about his experiences in the administration and the secret of his longevity in the upper echelons of public service. This late-night encounter in the stairwell marked the beginning of our monthly sessions in his office over the years that followed. This mentorship was especially appreciated by me because the agency I was responsible for was attached to the President's civil office, then led by Dr. Ibrahima Khalil Kaba. Dr. Kaba, a brilliant mathematician and former university professor in the United States, is known for his simplicity, diligence in work, and pragmatism. I had a familial, friendly, and professional relationship with "Lilou," as his close ones call him, which continued after his appointment to the presidency. Through him, I already had the opportunity to provide my opinion and propose solutions to issues that he and other members of the cabinet would seek my input on. His support was crucial in what I was able to achieve at the presidency. Kiridi and Khalil, along with other cabinet members, effectively played their roles as mentors and advisors to the young, hopeful, and energetic person that I was in an environment that could have its destructive surprises for a career that had just begun. Without them, the fruits would not have held the promise of the flowers.

2

A new cabinet for economic recovery

I did not count my time. I enjoyed participating actively in this Herculean project of changing my country's destiny, moving every day from one task to another, from one field to another. I could not hope for less. For a private sector executive, accustomed to tight deadlines and strict professional requirements, I had no trouble overcoming the risk of idleness that I foresaw and apprehended when entering the administration. Almost at the same time as me, other young executives had returned from abroad or left the local private sector to serve the country within the administration, as part of the approach of the Head of State to rejuvenate and modernize our administration, by calling on Guineans in the diaspora. These relatively young executives with a profile different from the typical profile of current civil servants were part of this wave that a diplomat proudly called "the Alpha generation", in reference to President Alpha Condé. We were not another kind of Guineans, we were simply Guineans, like all other administration employees, but with a different background. "See, like you, I have young Guineans who can speak English, come from the same schools as you and have international experience," the President often enjoyed saying to the foreign investors he would meet. He seemed to have the ambition to inject new blood into the system. The positions of advisers, less risky for a first experience in administration, seemed to constitute a first step.

After the legislative elections of September 28, 2013, the usual negotiations for the formation of the government took place. Speculation was rife about whether Prime Minister Mohamed Said Fofana[8] would stay. In fact, the Head of State had decided to re-appoint him and initiate the formation of the new government. I was far from the related discussions and kept working on the priority projects entrusted to me. It was therefore with great surprise that I received a call from a Chinese partner, a representative of a large mining company, one early morning in October 2013. He congratulated me on my future appointment as Minister of Mines and of Geology. It was easy to imagine his panic when I told him that I was unaware of this information. Given my proximity to the priority mining projects, it should logically make sense to me, especially since the city was buzzing with rumors of all kinds. However, I was astounded to hear it from the mouth of this usually cautious foreigner, and far from local rumors. On my way to my office, I took the initiative to call, whilst at the foot of the "Little Palace", a Botswanan friend with decades of experience in mining in her country and abroad. I told him about this rumor that I took seriously without realizing. Maybe I was just hoping it was true. "Now is not the right time yet," she replied, believing that I was "not ready for this position". My ego took a hit. Having received an unexpected setback, I gave myself time to collect my thoughts. I did not expect such a brutal and negative answer. Although shocked, I listened carefully to his explanation. I then arrived at my office and took half an hour to digest the shock of the announcement

[8] Prime minister of Guinea from December 2010 to December 2015.

of the Chinese gentleman, and the final opinion of my friend. Then, I resumed my daily tasks but refrained from discussing it with anyone. I learned, a few years later, without being able to verify its veracity, that the President had opened up to certain guests about his intention to appoint me to head the Ministry of Mines. Fortunately, if this intention existed at that time, it did not turn into a decision. I would probably not have lasted six months at the head of the Ministry of Mines had I been appointed in the new government at that moment. Indeed, after the first case in December 2013, the Ebola epidemic was officially declared on March 23, 2014 and did not end until December 29, 2015. These two years were extremely difficult for the Guinean economy, especially for mining. The history, the network, the experience of Kerfalla Yansané, appointed in January 2014 as Minister of Mines and Geology, have certainly enabled him to hold on for two years amid a health crisis and almost without investment, where a young minister unknown to the public would perhaps not have held. Despite the difficulties linked to the epidemic, with more rigor, Minister Yansané contributed to advancing the reform agenda in the sector.

In any case, I invested myself fully, during the two years that followed, in my activities which became increasingly concentrated on the mines, partly because of my functions, but also because of the will of the Minister of Mines to promote more active and constructive collaboration with the President's advisers on the projects of his department.

The closer we got to the presidential election, scheduled for October 2015, the more attention was focused on the preparation for this deadline. The regime's goal was to secure victory in the first round, a goal that was confirmed a few days after the vote with 57.85% of the votes for President Alpha Condé. This was followed by the traditional swearing-in ceremony and the appointment of the Prime Minister, head of the government, Mr. Mamady Youla[9], on December 26, 2015, before the formation of the new government.

The government led by Mamady Youla, a technocrat coming from the mining industry after a career in public administration, was formed on January 4, 2016. It comprised 31 ministers and 2 secretaries-general. About a third of the government consisted of individuals in their forties, most in their early forties. Many of them had studied abroad, worked in the private companies, or in international institutions in Guinea or abroad. A significant number were fluent in a second foreign language, usually English. Apart from a few who engaged in political activism from their adolescence, they were more professionals from various socio-economic sectors than politicians. This rejuvenation was certainly not a coincidence. It seemed to be the culmination of an initiative undertaken by the President for several years. One that brought some of these young professionals into his cabinet, the Prime Minister's office, or major state agencies. It aimed at refreshing the government to better understand and manage relations with the local private players, investors, and international partners and financiers. This was to increase the chances of success for the government's primary mission under Youla: the revival of a Guinean economy deeply affected by the Ebola epidemic.

[9] Prime minister of Guinea from December 2015 to May 2018.

3

Minister of Mines: " Do you have broad enough shoulders for the position " ?

One October afternoon in 2015, I received a call from the President requesting an immediate meeting. Expecting a discussion on a dossier under my responsibility, I was surprised that it involved reviewing the list of participants in a foreign mission in a field that did not directly concern me. As was his custom regarding foreign missions, he was concerned about the cost of Guinea's participation in this conference. Later, I realized that my input on this matter might have been a pretext for him to ask two or three suggestive yet crucial questions, ensuring that I was ready to take on significant responsibilities.

Leaving the *Sékhoutouréya* Presidential Palace, I had the idea that he might be considering appointing me as Minister of Mines. Nothing was certain, but I now had to consider this possibility. Did he intentionally prepare me for it, or was he still understandably uncertain, given that he was about to appoint a relatively unknown figure to one of the most important positions in the government? I could not know for sure. Nevertheless, I decided not to take any chances. I immediately began preparing for it, dedicating myself to crafting a roadmap for the effective assumption of my potential new responsibilities. This involved reviewing the sector's strategic orientations, its current situation, the challenges it faced, the working principles I needed to adopt for successful reforms, the approach I should infuse into my actions, priority objectives and actions, as well as the contribution of the mines to national priorities. In short, I documented everything I needed to succeed in what could become my next mission.

As the weeks passed, a certain rumor about my possible appointment as the head of the Ministry of Mines began to spread. Fortunately, many did not believe it. On my part, I obviously did not say a word to anyone, especially not to those seeking confirmation of what was merely a hypothesis in my eyes. As a precaution and out of respect for the incumbent minister, I ceased my visits, despite their regularity, to the ministry.

A few sincere individuals and many opportunists posing as kingmakers, stumbling upon a conversation about the growing rumor, informed me about all the activities surrounding the formation of the government. Some claimed to have information that turned out to be false, while others swore they could secure my appointment as a minister. I listened to everyone out of courtesy and respect. All this back-and-forth disturbed my usual activities, now compounded by my preparation for a potential government appointment. I kept my feet on the ground and revealed nothing. The passing weeks were long but enlightening.

The country was still officially in a state of Ebola epidemic, even though the situation was now under control, with hopes of an imminent announcement of the official end of the epidemic. This announcement was made on December 29, 2015. Five days later, on Monday, January 4, 2016, after a weekend filled with impatience and apprehension, the 33 members of Prime Minister Mamady Youla's government were appointed. Sitting in front of the national television, I had the confirmation of the long-awaited news: I was appointed as the Minister of Mines and Geology at the age of 39, an age considered "young," albeit erroneously, in a country unaccustomed to entrusting high positions to individuals—especially women—under the age of 40. While I was prepared for this eventuality, I was less prepared for the profile of the government members, including several individuals in their forties who had mostly evolved outside political circles. "People who have everything to lose if they fail," as the President's Agriculture Advisor, the late El Hadj Thierno Mamadou Cellou Diallo, known as "old Cellou," used to say in support of the rejuvenation of the cabinet. Even though I refrain from any fetishism about promoting youth, with merit being the primary criterion, it was evidently a certain renewal in the governance of the country.

Before having time to settle into my new role, I had to respond to all the expressions of pride and support from my close ones, old and new friends, and those who had just discovered connections buried for decades, if not nonexistent. I was not surprised by this influx of new acquaintances; nor was I fooled. Most people approached the minister, not Abdoulaye Magassouba. After this flood of calls, messages, and visits, I finally had the time to focus on my program for the first weeks. In my mind, I had to set the tone from the very beginning. I had to hit the ground running.

We began the preparations for the handover ceremony, which took place on Thursday, January 7, 2016. As usual, my family, friends, and colleagues were present. Beyond the customary thanks, I wanted to honor the outgoing minister, Kerfalla Yansané, for the reforms he initiated despite the extremely difficult situation created by the Ebola epidemic, which the sector endured during his two years at the helm. I wanted to honor him for serving the country for decades, even during very challenging periods for Guinea. I wanted to do it as openly as possible. In the middle of my speech, I called for a standing ovation for him. No work is perfect. His was no exception, as would be the case when I left the ministry. However, unlike some habits of systematically and indiscriminately casting blame on former high officials, throwing out the baby with the bathwater, I believe that the sacrifice of those who serve the country should be recognized while there is still time.

As for me, I fulfilled this duty with pleasure. And I made it a point, throughout my time in these roles, never to take credit for the work done by my predecessors or criticize their actions. I simply conducted an objective examination of the situation. On this basis, I continued everything that was well done in the interest of the country, corrected what needed to be corrected, while opening new avenues. Even though I had to bring a new dynamic to the leadership of the ministry, even though I had to adopt my own method and principles, I did not arrive on virgin territory. Work had been done. A foundation on which I had to build.

I immediately set to work on the finalization, now immersed, of the six-month work plan. In the ministry's functioning, measures had to be taken to improve what needed improvement in the working environment, while observing the behavior of each collaborator in a working situation.

Failure was not an option. Faced with the honor of serving, the understandable doubt of some, and the discontent or frustration of others, faced with expectations, I had to respond with concrete results. And quickly. When a journalist, whom I could not suspect of any negative intention, asked me, "Do you have broad enough shoulders for this position?" I responded, thinking that only results would matter, "We will judge by the outcome." I reject any form of nepotism or favoritism, any approach that would seek to favor friends and relatives solely based on personal connections. I reject it as much as the notion that family or friendship ties could be a hindrance for deserving individuals. At the time, defense or justification actions might have seemed useful. Actually, they would have been futile. The only right response, the one that would be effective, was to get to work and accelerate the development of the mines to demonstrate results, not just words.

4

Urgent projects

The top priority was to complete the main reforms as soon as possible. In such circumstances, there is no doubt about the need to implement reforms in a sector like mining. However, when the reform process takes a long time, it produces the unintended effect of creating permanent uncertainty about the final investment conditions. The investment environment and conditions were to be stabilized at the end of the reforms, which were no longer expected to last. We tackled two key elements of the system: the review of mining agreements and titles and the modernization of the mining cadaster.

The review of mining conventions and titles was initiated in March 2012, in line with an electoral promise by the candidate, President Alpha Condé, echoing a popular demand strongly expressed during the general strikes of January-February 2007 in Guinea[10]. The system was built around a technical committee with stakeholders, including civil society, and a strategic committee made up of ministers from the fields concerned. Together with the

[10] The 2007 Guinean general strike began on January 10, 2007 and ended on February 27, 2007. They were initiated by Guinea's trade unions.

chairman of the technical committee and its members, we picked up the pace and completed the review process on April 19, 2016.

In addition to completing this contract review, the reform of the mining cadaster was of pressing urgency. Despite the efforts of my predecessor, including the temporary closure of the cadaster to guarantee the integrity of the process of switching to the new system, the reform could not be completed. The long-time support of the World Bank[11] made it possible to have the resources to achieve this. The cadastral system—or should I say the cadastral systems—in force did not yet make it possible to know the exact number of permits. As soon as I took office, I asked the service in charge of the mining cadaster for the exhaustive list and the count of granted permits. I was outraged that conflicting numbers were given to me from one week to another, varying from 1,600 to 2,000. In fact, the directorate in charge of the mining cadaster was not able to provide an exact number on the simple and grotesque grounds that several databases of mining permits were active! The two main clans formed within the directorate each had their own base, their "clients" holding the permits, which they watched like milk on the stove. It took six months and the replacement of the two directors to finally know the exact number of permits, which was actually… 616! Very far from the initial figures. Collecting data as trivial as the number of permits was a state affair. With the lack of basic clarity and integrity, it was not only possible to have an overlap of permits (we had a few instances of this) but also for the site coordinates of a permit to refer, as in a few cases that

---

[11] Guinea - Mining Sector Governance Support Project. Washington, D.C. : World Bank Group. http://documents.worldbank.org/curated/en/272061468029370675/Guinea-Mining-Sector-Governance-Support-Project

we saw, to a location outside of the Guinean territory. With this finding, it was important for the cadastral team to include an information systems specialist to support the migration to a new single cadastral system, preserving data integrity, while the mining technicians took care of the establishment of a new, more precise, and more transparent cadastral procedure. After several months of effort, the modernization of the mining cadaster was completed in September 2016, then put online on the Internet in March 2017, about three years after the launch of the reform. Once the cadaster was online, the consolidation work had to be continued by canceling all inactive permits. In 2016, more than 200 permits were withdrawn. The last phases of this consolidation concerned permits for which there was neither an address nor a holder presenting himself to the services to safeguard their rights. Despite the persistent search for these holders by a bailiff, and the announcement in the media, no holder showed up. I learned later that these permits were presumably held by people, including government officials, under the cover of an assumed name, who obviously did not dare to come forward. It made sense that none of the holders filed a claim, despite the outright withdrawal of the permits. The watchword that we applied from now on was simple: any inactive license must be withdrawn.

Permit processing became more transparent and seamless, reducing the processing time for applications from three months to two weeks, on a first-come, first-served basis. The new procedure, widely published, set out the requirements which, once fulfilled, allowed the acceptance of the request, which was recorded and published on the online cadaster site, to avoid that another company could file a request on the same location. This request was processed by the team in charge of the cadaster, which then submitted it to a committee including other departments of the ministry. It is only after this committee has ruled that the file was submitted for the minister's signature. The procedure now provided for stricter verification of the technical and financial capacities of the applicant and of the administrative file upstream. This verification did not give the absolute guarantee that the project will be developed in strict compliance with the regulations; this task being the responsibility of the monitoring and control process put in place. However, it aimed at strengthening the filter at the entrance, thus giving more chances for project implementation. This mechanism made it possible to improve, over the years, the quality of permit holders and, above all, to create more jobs and investments in the industry. We could estimate that more than 2,000 new direct jobs were created on exploration permits during the years following this reform. This is comparable to the number of jobs created by an industrial operation of a certain size.

The analysis of evolution of the mining cadaster since the end of the initial consolidation of the base in September 2016 confirmed the trends expected from the reform implementation. There is indeed a drop in the total number of mining titles by 7%, from 616 in September 2016 to 570 in November 2020 and a drop in the number of exploration permits by 13%, from 539 to 471 between 2016 and 2020. This drop means that the State withdrew more permits over this period than it granted.

In addition to the application of the new procedure, this decrease is also attributable to the strengthening of monitoring, documentary control, and on-site control of permits. These controls made it possible to withdraw exploration permits each time violations of the regulations were observed. Indeed, more than 500 exploration permits were withdrawn during my tenure as the head of the ministry. The impact of controls on evolution of the number of permits showed a drop in speculative behavior. Unlike research permits, the number of operating permits increased by 15%, from 62 in September 2016 to 71 in November 2020, revealing that more projects were reaching maturity, moving from the exploration phase to the development phase. This was consistent with the growth in investments over this period following basic reforms (Mining Code, cadaster, EITI, etc.) and promotion efforts. This trend, with fewer permits subject to speculation, was also valid for mining concessions, increasing from 15 in September 2016 to 28 in November 2020.

Although the work of reviewing the mining contracts and reforming the cadaster occupied a good part of my time and that of the ministry team during the first months, other urgent matters of no lesser priority occupied our attention. The mining vision was translated into the provisions of the Mining Code adopted in 2011 and revised in 2013. My former duty in the presidency and my multiple interactions with the Head of State allowed me to better understand the motivations and objectives that underpinned the texts. I, therefore, took in hand the ministry's urgent projects and priorities based on the economic recovery mission assigned to the government, on my understanding of the sector's realities and challenges, as well as on my professional experience. All these allowed me to have a compass and to set benchmarks in strategy, principles, and method of action. To achieve this, resources were needed, of which the ministry team was the first.

5

A committed and dedicated team

We succeed only with a competent, efficient, and united team sharing a common vision and project. The prerequisite for everything is the understanding and adoption of the leader's approach and governance style by their collaborator. Therefore, I scheduled my first cabinet meeting immediately after taking office. On this occasion, I explained that I intended to work with each collaborator without prejudices, 'without looking back,' judging them based on their performance. Fairness in the treatment of my collaborators, rigor and efficiency in work, responsibility in resource management, and dialogue would govern the actions I would undertake with my collaborators. The rules were clear, and those who adhered to them would be my most appreciated collaborators, while others would face appropriate sanctions. Pedagogically, I explained each rule and listened to all observations. The tone was set. Everyone knew there would be no witch hunt. Only commitment to work and results mattered. At the end of the meeting, I asked each department to provide me with a report on the current situation. It should cover activities, resources, challenges faced, and proposals for the proper functioning of the department and the achievement of results.

It was crucial to reassure the collaborators so that each person's potential could be expressed without any subjective restraint, without any inhibition. Most of the senior executives in the ministry, like in other ministries, had well surpassed the age of fifty. I took advantage of this initial interaction to share with them the factual observation that youth is not eternal. It is a state of mind, a behavior. Based on this, I only intended to judge individuals based on their actions, without gratuitously favoring or opposing any generation. I emphasized that we are all Guineans, with the same rights and duties, regardless of age. I concluded that my role was not to blindly replace the fathers of some Guineans with the sons of others. I have always believed that despite any criticisms directed at certain older executives in the administration, the state had not done enough to guarantee a career plan and a minimum of professional and financial security, granting the full right to circumscribe, if not banish, certain behaviors that, while reprehensible, were partially explainable by shortcomings in the treatment of the civil servant; who represents the linchpin in the functioning of the state. I did not claim to change this endemic situation, but I promised myself to be fair. I promised to have empathy and consideration for the working conditions and, to some extent, the living conditions of the civil servants I was responsible for leading.

From the very beginning, I felt that I had somewhat started to create an atmosphere of serenity to engage in the battle, the only one worth fighting for: the development of the mines. My initial intention was to propose appointments to leadership positions to the Head of State within two to three weeks of my appointment. It would have been hasty and adventurous. After seeking the advice of more experienced individuals, including some former ministers, I realized it was better to take my time. I overestimated my level of knowledge of the ministry's executives, even though I had worked with some of them while handling mining issues in my previous position. Judging by actions necessarily required taking some time. The six months following my appointment would provide me with all the elements I needed to make informed choices and propose them. I observed all my collaborators in action during these months. Then, I chose a few individuals with no interest in the appointments to reflect on a better organization of the ministry, review the CVs of the executives, and formulate proposals for different positions. I made it a point to promote all the ministry's executives who made sincere and productive efforts to advance the agenda of reforms and project development during the first few months, which unfolded at a frenetic pace with days rarely ending before ten in the evening. This resonated perfectly with my intention to be just and fair, to promote merit, to the extent possible. My intention was to create a team composed of a mix of experienced senior executives, to which young executives with high potential would be added to ensure succession. In almost all departments, one of the two leadership positions was thus to be held by a relatively young executive. In addition to refreshing in terms of dynamism, this allowed for the preparation of the next generation of directors in a logic of renewal in continuity, ensuring the sustainability of the dynamic. To counteract the lingering trauma of a wave of appointments of individuals parachuted in from outside by one of my distant predecessors, most of the appointed executives were active within the ministry. The promise not to conduct a witch hunt was also kept, reassuring the entire staff that appointments were based on the quality of work, potential, experience, and merit.

After the restructuring of the ministry, the establishment of the new team on July 8, 2016, marked the beginning of a new dynamic for which we fought to maintain in the following years. We immediately worked to build trust with all stakeholders, internal and external, to enable the ministry to fully exercise its responsibilities in a transparent, rigorous, and reliable framework. In this arrangement, strict adherence to the hierarchical order, unlike some practices, was observed to ensure the normal and effective functioning of the departments. My only contacts, in the context of work, were the secretary-general, the chief of staff, advisors, directors, and their deputies. It was important to ensure that directors were fully responsible for the operation of the departments they were in charge and accountable of the results achieved by these departments. Any collaborators who tried, without the knowledge of their hierarchical boss, to establish a direct relationship with me quickly realized it was not possible. Collaborators had the opportunity to exchange with me if their directors decided to involve them in a meeting or during the large meetings, I organized every month. These meetings were an opportunity to share information on all ministry issues with all executives, answer their questions, and gather their comments and suggestions. The goal was to ensure that ministry executives, assumed to be informed citizens, embraced the reform agenda for the sake of efficiency at work and had all the information about the sector to be the primary information channels.

To ensure efficiency, transparency, and traceability in the management of files, all were handled by technical services and advisors, without any exception. No technical file of the ministry was ever handled at my level alone. This also aimed to ensure the normal functioning of all services and the mastery of cases, results, and difficulties by all collaborators within the technical services. Also, unlike the practice where cabinet meetings are held only under the minister's direction, this weekly instance of information sharing and contribution to decisions was held under the direction of the highest-ranking official present (particularly the secretary-general or chief of staff in the absence of the minister). It was important for me that it was not 'my ministry' but rather 'the Ministry of Mines of the Republic.' I systematically corrected all correspondence that presented the ministry as the property of the department head. This mode of operation, which I consider normal, was meant to contribute to strengthening the institution, ensuring better involvement of staff, and thus perpetuating the achievements that I would have facilitated during my time at the helm of the ministry.

I demanded absolute loyalty to the mission entrusted to the ministry, to well-done work, and not to my person. I consistently applied the open-door policy, not requiring ministry executives to request an audience, but every meeting had to be dedicated to the needs of the service, not to gossip and other endemic denunciations within the administration.

Despite some regrettable actions by a few over the years and a certain decline in team productivity for various reasons, most ministry executives worked to advance reforms and projects.

6

Modernization, a priority in the reforms

Teams can only be effective in the long term if they operate within an appropriate governance framework, equipped with the necessary resources, and means to achieve the assigned objectives. From December 2014 to December 2015, the Ministry of Mines underwent an institutional audit conducted by the KPMG firm, with the support of the World Bank. Upon assuming office, I tasked a team with reviewing this report, with the assistance of the auditing firm that we re-engaged for this purpose. The initial focus was on extracting the main recommendations and proposing a restructuring of the ministry based on this.

The new organization was implemented on April 20, 2016. It acknowledged the consideration of critical issues of the industry, including the necessity of infrastructure development, a bottleneck in the development of bauxite and iron projects, as well as the management of community relations and the promotion of local content.

From the outset, the modernization of the ministry was initiated, particularly to fully leverage information and communication technologies. A ministry that lacked a website and even basic connectivity at its headquarters!

This anomaly was corrected within the first month. The establishment of a website provided greater visibility and ease of access to information for all stakeholders and observers within the framework of the ongoing transparency agenda. The introduction of a permanent Internet connection gave us the right to demand that collaborators be more responsive and efficient in the processing and sharing of information. With continuous support from the revitalized IT department, even colleagues who had never touched a computer began to familiarize themselves with information technology to the extent that we now had an average response time that did not exceed an hour.

Modernization continued to progress over the months and years. The development of the IT master plan formalized this process. In addition to the modernization of the mining cadaster management system, we digitized the quarry monitoring system through the electronic quarry management application. This allowed for better control of operational data, including a mobile application with geolocation used by all field agents on the smartphones provided to them.

Another information management challenge in the mines was the periodic collection of statistical information from mining companies. In addition to multiple requests from the Ministry of Mines and other departments, leading to unnecessary workload for the companies, we faced a perpetual delay in collecting and processing information, including sector production data crucial for performance evaluation. The Mining Information Collection Application (ACIM) helped overcome this obstacle. We now had a platform where focal points in companies, trained for this purpose across the country, could enter quarterly data on production, revenue, local content, etc. In addition to reducing the workload for companies, we were equipped to produce the eagerly awaited Mining Statistics Bulletin (quarterly). We managed to significantly reduce the Bulletin's production time while improving its quality, quarter after quarter.

The latest project in the dematerialization process focused on Electronic File Management. This application created the conditions for the complete dematerialization of the administrative process, allowing for effective and total telecommuting, and, most importantly, efficiency in processing files while ensuring effectiveness in archiving and file retrieval. The electronic archiving project, in its final implementation phase, is expected to complete this undertaking.

In parallel with this modernization process, the various departments were gradually equipped with work materials. The modernization process will be sustained through the maintenance and improvement of existing systems, as well as the implementation of all short, medium, and long-term actions outlined in the IT master plan. An important step will eventually be the establishment of an integrated management system that consolidates all applications to cover all areas of ministry action.

7

Better capacities, practices and working conditions

The strengthening of the capacities of executives has often been extended to other administrations involved in mining projects (public works, economy and finance, budget, territorial administration, and decentralization, etc.) to account for the integrated and transversal nature of mining projects. It covered all subjects of interest to the mining sector. In addition to individual training, the ministry conducted no less than 3,000 man-days of training between 2016 and 2020, equivalent to a full month of training for 100 executives. In April 2016, we relaunched the training program, with the support of the African Development Bank. This comprehensive program covered nine modules, each lasting five days, for about fifty executives. The themes covered understanding, mastering, and anticipating mining projects, addressing technical, commercial, legal, and financial issues at each phase. Several other training sessions were initiated by the ministry, particularly for strengthening the control and monitoring capacities of mining activities. More flexibly, on-demand training was carried out as part of a fair arbitration mechanism by a committee set up for this purpose. To maintain momentum during the Covid-19 pandemic, we implemented a special program for management and leadership training for all senior executives of the ministry with the National School of Public Administration of Canada (ENAP). In addition to addressing managerial shortcomings, this training was part of our strategy to prepare the ministry to be more effective for the post-Covid-19 period, to offset the impacts of the pandemic on mining activities. ENAP also supported the ministry in developing a comprehensive training program for the department based on the short and medium-term development plan for the mining sector.

These capacity-building efforts were accompanied by an improvement in the working conditions of the ministry's staff. At the central and decentralized levels, we built or rehabilitated about fifty offices, with auxiliary facilities. In this context, the program to construct the buildings of regional and prefectural directorates of mines and geology was initiated. The localities of Boké, Kankan, Siguiri, and Dinguiraye saw the completion of this project, which is of capital importance for a sector whose activities are deployed in the interior of the country and not in Conakry. In the same concern for improving working conditions, all central directorates and some decentralized directorates were provided with means of transportation to ensure the mobility of personnel. Creating better working conditions in the interior of the country is critical for the development of the country's mines. This creates proximity to mining activities in the context of their support, monitoring, and field control.

The available capacities can only be effective in a framework whose standards are known to all and effectively applied. This is why we initiated an organizational review and the development of procedure manuals for the National Agency for Mining Infrastructure Development (ANAIM), the Mining Investment Fund

(FIM), and the Ministry of Mines and Geology. This process should be followed by the periodic evaluation of the effective implementation of the procedure manuals at the level of each institution and the ministry, whose operations manual has also been developed. Capacity building, improving working conditions, and implementing more standardized and effective management systems had to be complemented by a change in practices to avoid that reforms remain mere wishes. However, it is customary that in the resistance to change, some actors take refuge in the comfort of established habits. "We've always done it this way" is often heard. The discomfort created by change and the challenge to established interests or other advantages are often the cause of resistance, whether passive or active. Keeping this in mind, I adopted an approach that was as educational and transparent as possible, aiming to isolate the most resistant — thus exposing their bad faith — while remaining open to suggestions, to ensure the feasibility and relevance of the changes.

One of the practices that persisted in the ministry concerned the coverage of its mission expenses by mining companies, including in the case of control or investigation missions. We made the coverage of mission expenses by the ministry systematic to ensure better independence. Periodic missions were carried out in all prefectures to verify compliance with the commitments attached to permits and authorizations. We usually carried out two each year. At the end of each of these missions, a verification was carried out by the inspectorate general of mines, which was free to take a sample to confirm that the results of the mission were not biased or altered. Then, we systematically withdrew all permits that were recommended for withdrawal. The prohibitive shortcomings often related to the unjustified absence of activities in the field or non-payment of surface taxes (these taxes owed to communities, the non-payment of which discredits the sector at its base). For a long time, permits were more used as mere speculative instruments by holders who had never visited their sites and sometimes had no idea where their perimeters were. However, the watchword was clear: any inactive permit must be withdrawn, regardless of the holder. The systematic application of this watchword has created hundreds, if not thousands, of jobs on permits whose holders were active in recruiting personnel to do the work in the field. This has also helped to reduce the number of unscrupulous and speculative investors in the mines to make way for more serious investors. From only 12 companies in the exploration phase in 2010, the sector grew to 43 in 2015, then to 340 in 2019.

Despite hundreds of permits being withdrawn over the years, the State has never been sued by an investor. The robustness of the verification process at multiple levels before the validation of mission reports certainly helped make the result of this process difficult to contest.

In addition to periodic missions, surprise missions were often organized with technical services or the inspectorate general of mines, based on information from various sources or even press articles. Any credible information was verified to ensure that unscrupulous permit holders had little chance of escaping control and legal sanctions.

In general, we have strengthened controls at various levels to exert pressure on permit holders, compelling them to fulfill their obligations. Among these controls, there were those concerning the mandatory repatriation of currencies from artisanal gold exports. When we initiated the control of repatriations by export counters in April 2016, we found that only 42% of the revenues from export counters were repatriated. We issued a formal notice to about forty counters in service. After a certain period, and realizing that many of them did not believe that we would go all the way and had engaged in aggressive lobbying, we wanted to reaffirm our absolute firmness. An information meeting was an opportunity to make them understand that any counter that did not comply would really lose its license. Eleven licenses were eventually withdrawn at the end of the additional period granted to all counters. The level of repatriation of currencies from exports increased from 42% before 2016 to over 90% in the following years. This helped support the stability of the Guinean franc, especially with significant repatriations amounting to nearly a billion dollars in 2017. These repatriations, distinct from the revenues collected by the State, represent the turnover of private operators (the counters) who exported gold and directly received these amounts in their accounts in the Guinean banking system. Therefore, these are private revenues of the counters and not public revenues at the disposal of the State.

On another front, we initiated the process of controlling the quantities and quality of exported products. Quantity control activities effectively began in June 2018, with a series of theoretical and practical training sessions for personnel in Guinea and abroad, with the support of German cooperation (GIZ)[12]. From January 2019 to December 2020, the quantity assessors' team conducted controls on the quantities of 1,470 shipments. At the end of 2019, the difference between the quantities declared by companies (69.821 million tonnes) and those sampled by the ministry's assessors (69.826 million tonnes) was less than 0.01%. While I completely acknowledge the necessity and deterrent nature of quantity control, my personal conviction has always been that the absence of

12 https://www.giz.de/en/downloads/giz2022-en-regional-resource-governance-west-africa.pdf

control partly fueled the fantasy that entire ships had left incognito, even escaping the vigilance of customs officials present in the ports. This possibility, although not entirely dismissible, seemed exaggerated to me for bulk ore exported by ships of tens of thousands of tonnes, especially since international trade data generally allow free access to the quantities received by the ports of destination. Clearly, a bauxite ship is not a nugget of gold or a precious stone that smugglers can slip into a bag or pocket to pass through airport security.

Quality control, unlike quantity control, faced delays in implementation, primarily because of the requirement to build or renovate a geological analysis laboratory. As part of a public/private partnership, we were able to rehabilitate and equip the National Geological Laboratory, and train the staff, in Guinea and India; an unprecedented investment (reconstruction and equipment) for several decades. This investment, and others in progress, enable Guinea to have the necessary capacities to also cover the quality control of exports, to ensure that the declared grades correspond effectively to reality for the calculation of mining taxes and monitoring of deposit exploitation.

The changes in practices, in procedures, have accelerated the reform agenda. They were not easy since some habits, decades-old, are deeply rooted within the administration. While it is understandable that civil servants may have difficulty accepting the necessary changes, I was somewhat surprised by the reaction of some companies accustomed to preferential treatment. Lies, intimidations, threats, and other dirty tricks abound when the interests of some are threatened.

I remember a project promoter who deceived his financial partner and sent me a long letter with insults of all kinds to claim rights that belonged to his partner. I, of course, refrained from responding, following my principle of systematically refusing any emotional reaction with investors. Eventually, he came to seek an amicable resolution, which we granted without difficulty. He then continued peacefully developing his project with his financial partner. He later explained that he had experienced practices in a certain past that he did not imagine were outdated. Indeed, some investors, who had become accustomed to enjoying preferential treatment in a distant past, believed they could prosper with the same practices. Some of them did not hesitate to try to bypass the ministry's procedures and engage in strong interventions in the field, media blackmail, and all forms of accusations against the ministry. The allocation of certain mines was the subject of numerous sometimes illegal acts. Some candidates for the allocation of a mine pushed the community hosting that mine to physically attack, or even lynch, any other investor who would come to visit the facilities. Ministry staff, with a mission order, who accompanied another investor, only survived because they quickly spoke the local dialect and miraculously managed to reason with the youths ready to fight with various weapons. Regular threats of all kinds, including death threats, were made in the context of the allocation of another mine. Not to mention the constant pressures from all sides and in all forms to obtain favors in the allocation of the deposit. I made it a point to make it clear to all possible sources of threats, attempts at intimidation, and pressure that we only allocate deposits based on the objective evaluation of a technical committee, with the assurance that the best offer had been chosen.

The reform agenda within the ministry was made possible by a stronger mobilization of resources, another fruit of reinforced controls. In addition to internal resources, the ministry had been supported since 2012 by the Project to Support Governance in Mining, which, with the support of the World Bank, enabled the implementation of ambitious initiatives. This project was supplemented by the Project to Support the Strengthening of Administration Capacities for the Implementation of Integrated Mining Projects, with the support of the African Development Bank. The International Finance Corporation (IFC), UNDP, GIZ, and several other partners accompanied the reform at various levels.

Several reforms were carried out with other ministries due to the multisectoral nature of mining projects. A mining project is not a project of the Ministry of Mines but a project of the State, of the country, in its entirety. The lack of ownership of projects by different administrations has led to the bankruptcy of more than one. This ownership must go beyond ministers with whom, in general, we have had good collaboration and who, involved in the discussions preceding the signings (especially at the level of the council of ministers), are generally prompt in responding to the requests of the Ministry of Mines. This concerns, in particular, ministers from sectors most involved in mining (including territorial administration, budget, transportation, environment, and territorial planning). The same cannot be said for some officials within ministries who only make slow progress on the management of mining project development files. Some even sometimes express surprising opinions from people in charge of implementing the State's commitments. This is particularly striking as the commitments in the mining conventions are not those of the Ministry of Mines but rather the commitments of the entire government, which are binding on officials at all levels. These commitments are implemented by more than ten departments and agencies, in the case of integrated mining projects. These commitments are, moreover, adopted in a law that is binding on all. It is in this logic of multisectoral approach that a one-stop shop was set up in November 2017 for permits and authorizations for mining projects, with the support of the International Finance Corporation (IFC). Under the control of the Inter-ministerial Committee for the Monitoring of Integrated Mining Projects (CISPMI), made up of the ministries and agencies concerned by the said projects, the Permanent Secretariat of the CISPMI (acting as a one-stop shop) had set up a monitoring system and an information portal on permits and authorizations. In this system, the one-stop shop works upstream with mining projects, to identify the non-mining permits and authorizations needed to carry out the projects and plan the administrative procedures.

The complete operationalization of the one stop shop for integrated mining projects, the effective implementation of delegation of powers and simplification of procedures, and the sustainability of these instruments are the primary challenges to fully enable this one-stop shop to play its role durably. Beyond ministerial government solidarity, we must move towards solidarity across all administrations concerning mining projects, as their success contributes to achieving the goals of all departments in one way or another.

To achieve this, the Ministry of Mines must undoubtedly strengthen information and awareness at all levels of administration. Hence, we took the initiative to organize joint visits of officials from different ministries to mining projects, ensuring broader ownership of projects within the administration beyond the Ministry of Mines.

After several years of reforms, the ministry has gained in efficiency and productivity. The regulations provide for a lifespan of exploration permits for a period of up to seven years (including three years for the initial grant and two possible renewals of two years each). In practice, the exploration phase lasts at least three years in almost all cases on a virgin site. Following exploration, allowing the investor to have a commercially exploitable deposit, they initiate the development phase, involving the completion of feasibility and environmental and social impact studies. At the end of this development phase, which can last two years, the company mobilizes financing (equity and debts), a process that can take an additional two years. Only after that is the construction phase of the project initiated. This final phase generally takes no less than two to four years. In practice, it takes around ten years to go through all the phases of a mining project from launching the exploration phase to commencement of exploitation.

Thanks to the initiated reforms, we have been able to enhance administration efficiency and shorten project realization timelines. For instance, we successfully completed the construction phase of an integrated bauxite exploitation project in eighteen months, the railway project phase (initially planned for three years) in about two years, and the development, financing mobilization, and construction phases of a gold exploitation project in four years. Despite these achievements, there is still significant room for improvement since the reforms are far from complete. It is imperative that they be continued and consolidated in the coming years to make them effectively irreversible and the administration even more efficient.

8

The mining sector, a lever for economic development

The development of mines should not be viewed exclusively through the mining lens. It should be seen in the broader perspective of socio-economic development. My reflexes and my economist profile, rather than that of a technical expert in mining, have facilitated this holistic understanding of mining development from the outset. Mines are more of a "means" than an "end." I have often heard, especially in the months following my appointment, that Guinea should not be a “mining country”. That we have, for too long and wrongly, placed excessive hope on mining to develop Guinea. It is now necessary to focus on other sectors. This analysis, while not entirely incorrect, is a shortcut that can be misleading.

Firstly, each country must identify its areas of development opportunities in the short, medium, and long terms and use them as leverage to overcome obstacles effectively on the path to its development. Regardless of our wishes, Guinea needs substantial financial resources to develop the human capital and numerous infrastructures required for the development of its vast potential in sectors such as agriculture, tourism, livestock, industry, etc. An immediate opportunity to mobilize these financial resources is offered by mines in the case of Guinea. Mines, therefore, currently serve as a significant lever to set the country on the path of development. It is imperative that our development policy incorporates this constraint and turns it into a real asset. Any other option could be precarious. How can it be justified that the state abruptly loses interest in an industry that accounts for no less than 80% of its exports, a quarter of its revenue, 20% of its GDP, and over 90% of foreign direct investments? I spent part of my first year as a minister sensitizing certain members of the administration and international donors who were promoting the misguided idea of disengaging from investments in mining.

My conviction was particularly strengthened by the history of many developed countries such as Australia, France, Germany, the United States, Canada, etc. It was also reinforced by the genesis of the construction of the European Union around mining and industrial cooperation with the European Coal and Steel Community (ECSC), the first supranational community in Europe, which came into effect in 1952.

The history of the development of these countries and unions teaches us that mines can be a significant lever in economic development, in economic transformation, and integration. However, for mines to fully play this role, the country must have robust governance in the sector. This was not really the case in 2010 when the new regime was taking shape. However, a change in governance requires years of reforms to see its impact.

These countries, which have succeeded in their structural transformation through mining, first managed to establish governance that allowed them to make the most of the mines. In essence, this involves ensuring the responsible exploitation of mineral resources through socially and environmentally respectful practices, implementing good practices in terms of combating corruption and promoting transparency, managing mining revenues rationally, particularly in favor of economic diversification and investment in socio-economic infrastructure, better integrating mines into local and national economies, and creating local added value through processing, etc.

The necessity to make the most of the mines in Guinea implies, first and foremost, their exploitation through foreign direct investments. Neither the limited resources of the state nor the even more limited financial capacities of the national private players can cope with the substantial investments required by mining projects. These investments amount to tens or even hundreds of millions. Foreign investors, in their pursuit of profit, have always seemed interested in Guinean mines due to the size, diversity, and quality of Guinea's potential in this field. To attract them, the state had to create a favorable investment framework that guarantees them a return on investment within an acceptable timeframe.

Mining operations are expected to last for at least a decade of production, following an initial decade of investment in research, development, and construction. Investment and return on investment are therefore spread across several political cycles, creating a risk for the investor who is concerned that their rights may be challenged by a new regime or that their operations may be disrupted or even halted. Beyond the intentions of the leaders, the mining investor needs the country's institutions to provide a guarantee to safeguard their rights. This is why it is crucial for reforms to be deep and irreversible, outlasting the minister, the government, and the regime. Only then can the mining attract credible investors with mutually beneficial viable projects. Otherwise, the sector would essentially be overrun by adventurers with questionable credibility looking for short-term transactions or projects.

The goal is to use the mining industry as a lever to diversify the economy in the broadest sense and build accelerated inclusive growth. In this regard, three channels for capturing the benefits of the sector are prioritized.

The first channel involves the ***effective collection and rational use of mining revenues*** (current and future) to invest in inclusive growth beyond mining. In addition to investments made through traditional budgetary expenditures, the focus is on strategic investments in areas such as infrastructure, agriculture, energy, education, health, etc. As an example, the financing of the Kaléta hydroelectric dam (240 megawatts), with a state counterpart payment of $112 million, was covered through mining revenues. The same applies to the financing of projects under the Sino-Guinean framework agreement signed on September 5, 2017, aiming for a total investment of $20 billion over twenty years through an "enclave" loans mechanism. This mechanism is based on financing priority socio-economic infrastructure projects (transportation, energy, education, etc.), with repayment assured by mining revenues held with an agreed-upon bank. The total amount of $20 billion is not a loan contracted by Guinea at the signing of the framework agreement, nor is it a barter, as many thought at the time of signing the agreement with the Chinese authorities. It consists of a series of loans individually and separately contracted over an indicative period of twenty years, following established procedures, including the submission of financing agreements to parliament. These loans are repaid by revenues from mining projects implemented in accordance with the Mining Code, with individually negotiated agreements submitted to the Guinean Parliament. The only connection between the mining projects and the framework agreement is the state's choice to use mining revenues, once available, to repay loans contracted for the financing of basic socio-economic infrastructure. The construction contracts for the infrastructure are negotiated and signed by the entities involved in the procurement of works (the ministries responsible for Public Works and Finance, and the Administration of major projects). The role of the Ministry of Mines is limited to the implementation of mining projects according to the provisions of the Mining Code and sharing information related to future revenues. Financing agreements are negotiated and signed by the Ministry of Finance, which commits the State in this regard. The first two financing agreements signed under this cooperation covered the reconstruction of the national road on the Coyah-Mamou-Dabola section (370 km) and the rehabilitation/reconstruction of roads in Conakry (including the reconstruction of the 2×2 Novembre 8th Bridge-Bellevue Road) for a total amount of 515 million euros.

In addition to the framework agreement, mining revenues are used to directly finance critical infrastructure for the development of certain mining localities, as seen in the case of the Siguiri-Kintinian road (35 km) and the ongoing Boké bypass road project. This is not to mention the infrastructures and other projects carried out under the National Fund for Local Development (FNDL) and the Local Economic Development Fund (FODEL).

The impact of the rational use of mining revenues can only be significant if the collection of these revenues is effective and as comprehensive as possible. On this matter, the Ministry of Mines is often wrongly held accountable for the state's fiscal revenues. Even though it must ensure, as the supervisory authority, that investors adhere to their commitments, the role of the Ministry of

Mines is primarily concerned with the responsible development of mining activities, not the collection of fiscal revenues, let alone the use of these revenues.

The second channel involves ***maximizing economic impact through positive externalities***, particularly through integrated projects with multi-user infrastructure systems that support mining, agricultural, and other commercial activities to promote local content. This promotion of local content provides opportunities for local SMEs to access markets, enabling them to enhance their capabilities and sustainability. It also improves the availability of skilled local labor through recruitment, promotion, and capacity building. The benefits generated by mining activities can thus be disseminated to other sectors by creating wealth in these areas and utilizing new resources and capacities (SMEs and labor) nationally or internationally. This approach to maximizing impacts is valid at both the national and local levels. That is why the integrated local development strategy, developed as part of a pilot study in the Boké prefecture, should be extended to all active mining zones, with the aim of maximizing socio-economic development opportunities through the creation of other economic activities, related or unrelated to mining, in fields such as agriculture, livestock, fisheries, industry, energy, various infrastructures, etc., for sustainable and inclusive local development. In general, the state must make more efforts to enhance economic integration by creating greater synergy between the mining industry and other sectors of the economy. This should be considered in the development and implementation of public policies.

Finally, the third channel is the ***dissemination of the effects of the improvement in the investment framework in the mining sector*** on the overall business environment. These effects are disseminated due to the significance of the mining industry in the general perception of governance and the integrated nature of mining projects. The most complex of these mining projects directly involve more than a dozen ministries and public agencies, including public works, land planning, transportation, etc. Improving the business environment in mining can, therefore, influence investment in other sectors of the economy and, consequently, on growth and development beyond mining. Reforms have a positive impact on the performance of ministries and agencies involved in mining projects. The improvement in the perception of the mines, therefore, spills over into the investment perception in other sectors of the country. An improvement in this perception has a multiplier effect realized not only through related investments by mining companies but also through investments by new companies in other fields of the economy.

Despite all the benefits it can generate, the mining industry cannot solve all the country's problems. Therefore, through better utilization of the mining opportunity, the country must gradually become independent of the mining industry by accelerating its diversification. This independence is especially necessary because the highly capital-intensive mining industry is dependent on a fluctuating global market beyond Guinea's control. This uncertainty will persist until Guinea can transform much of its production for final consumption at the national, sub-regional, or regional levels. Despite the key role of mining in the country's socio-economic development for a few decades, the path to economic prosperity and resilience lies in an economy that is much less dependent on mining over the years. The more the country maximizes the impact of the sector through all the channels presented above, the more independent its economy will be from mining.

If the direct impacts of mines, though insufficient in meeting socio-economic needs, are visible, the indirect and induced impacts of mining activity are often underestimated since they are not always evident to capture comprehensively. To better understand these socio-economic impacts and draw appropriate lessons for mining policy, we conducted an independent assessment of the economic impact of the mining industry from March to August 2020, covering the period from 2011 to 2020. This assessment was carried out by the consulting firm MNH Consulting.

The synthesis of the evaluation results presented below provides a better response to the frequently heard question, which tends to carry a negative connotation: "*What are mines for?*" These results and additional information, which quantitatively largely addresses this question, are as follows:

- ***A nearly threefold increase in the number of active companies*** *and a twenty-eightfold increase in the number of companies in the exploration phase. The number of companies in the exploitation phase, which was six (6) in 2010, increased to seventeen (17) in 2020. This number of companies is expected to significantly increase over the next five years, considering the significant growth in companies in the exploration and development phases. The number of companies in the exploration phase increased from only 12 in 2010 to 43 in 2015 and then to 340 in 2019. This increase is more pronounced in gold (going from 8 to 256 companies) and bauxite (from only 1 to 65 companies).*
- *Reforms have made Guinea a preferred destination for mining investments in Africa, with a* ***total investment level of $6.4 billion*** *at an average annual rate of $640 million from 2011 to 2019. This unprecedented level of investment, of which $6.2 billion (nearly 97%) was*

realized between 2015 and 2020, is consistent with the positive evolution of the business environment. As an illustration, the 2015 report from the Fraser Institute (a Canada-based organization of reference) ranked Guinea 103rd globally and 20th in Africa in terms of attractiveness for mining investments. Thanks to reforms in the sector, the 2019 report from the same organization ranked Guinea 20th globally and 1st in Africa!

- ***Investments**, which were only $18 million in 2010, increased to reach $1.4 billion in 2020. Investments in the mines are, to a large extent, driven by those in the bauxite industry. Out of the total mining investments from 2011 to 2020, 87.9% come from the bauxite sector ($5.6 billion), and 12.1% from the gold sector ($776 million).*
- ***Mining investments have led to a fourfold increase in bauxite production**, making Guinea a major player in the global market. Bauxite production, which was 17 million tonnes in 2010, reached 21 million tonnes in 2015. From 2016, bauxite production intensified, reaching a record level of 70.2 million tonnes in 2019.*
- ***Nearly a doubling of gold production**, driven by both industrial and artisanal production. Gold production increased from 14.7 tonnes in 2010 to 26.8 tonnes in 2019. Industrial gold production remained generally stable, averaging 14.2 tonnes annually, thanks to new investments. Artisanal production increased from 4.9 tonnes in 2012 to 14.3 tonnes in 2019, notably due to the removal of taxes on artisanal gold exports.*
- *Because of the increase in mining production, the number of **jobs multiplied by 2.7** between 2010 and 2019. The total number of jobs, which was 19,016 in 2010, reached 50,854 in 2019. With an average household size of 6.6 people in mining areas (according to the 2018 Light Poverty Evaluation Survey, ELEP), it can be estimated that more than 335,000 Guineans directly benefit from*

industrial mining activities, not counting those benefiting from induced jobs, local purchases, and artisanal mining.

- *The number of* ***direct jobs in mining*** *almost tripled, increasing* ***from 6,110 in 2010 to 16,340 in 2019****. This increase, more pronounced from 2015 onward, is primarily attributed to the performance observed in the bauxite sector. Indirect jobs show a similar trend to direct jobs, with an estimated 34,515 jobs in 2019, compared to 12,906 in 2010.*
- *These jobs have generated* ***income for households*** *through the wage bill paid to workers, which multiplied by four between 2010 and 2019. The wage bill of the industry increased from 345 billion GNF in 2010 to* ***1,381 billion GNF (more than 150 million US dollars) in 2019****. This increase is driven by both gold and bauxite companies.*
- *The increase in mining production has also been an* ***opportunity for local businesses*** *through purchases of goods and services by mining companies. These purchases represented approximately 1.1% of the GDP between 2011 and 2019, reflecting their significant impact on national wealth creation. This weight even increased during the last two years, averaging 2.5%. Overall, these purchases are estimated at* ***8,030.9 billion GNF (approximately 900 million US dollars) between 2011 and 2019****, with an average annual amount of 892.3 billion GNF. With the continued implementation of the local content promotion policy, especially through the Suppliers Subcontracting and partnership Marketplace (BSTP), these local purchases and mining services are expected to improve in the coming years.*
- ***Mining activity has significantly contributed to the state budget*** *over the period 2011-2019: direct mining public revenues were $397 million USD in 2019, compared to only $115 million USD in 2010. It is important to note that these revenues only cover the direct*

income received by the state from companies with mining titles, without taking into account revenues from subcontracting companies, which owe their existence to mining operations and investments. Furthermore, reports from the Extractive Industries Transparency Initiative (EITI) show that the overall revenues generated by the mining industry almost doubled between 2015 and 2018, increasing from $293 million USD to $544 million USD.

- *Mining has become a **significant source of funding for local communities**, in line with the presidential vision. The creation of the National Agency for Local Government Financing (ANAFIC), responsible for financing through the National Local Development Fund (FNDL), and the Local Economic Development Fund (FODEL) has been crucial in the process of local development in our country. ANAFIC (FNDL) resources represent 15% of sector taxes mobilized by the state and are intended for all communities. FODEL resources represent 0.5% or 1% of the turnover of companies for communities hosting mining activities. Thanks to these reforms, resources mobilized for local community financing reached 324.5 billion GNF (approximately 40 million US dollars) between 2011 and the first quarter of 2020, with an average annual amount of 29.6 billion GNF, compared to only 1.1 billion in 2010.*
- *Resources from mining have funded a **significant number of basic socio-economic infrastructures and businesses** in communities. In total, 606 development infrastructures have been financed by these resources. These infrastructures include, among others, over 200 classrooms, 140 wells, 81 health facilities, 14 bridges and crossing structures, 31 kilometers of rural roads, and 31 youth centers. These mining revenues allocated to communities have also funded the activities of 3,477 livestock breeders and 1,380 fishermen.*

• *Mining operations* ***contribute significantly to reducing poverty incidence****. Individuals in mining areas are less likely to be poor than those in non-mining localities. Indeed, the probability for an individual residing in a mining area to be poor is 13.7%. This risk is equal to 26.8% for a person in a locality bordering a mining area and 30.3% for an individual living in a non-mining locality and not bordering a mining area. In other words, the risk for a person to be poor in a non-mining area and not bordering a mining area is three times higher than for an individual residing in a mining area. This result is consistent with the exponential migration flow observed towards mining areas, revealing the existence of economic opportunities created within and around mining operations (even though it creates demographic pressure exacerbating the deficit of basic social services).*

• *Mining has also become an* ***engine of economic growth*** *and a source of economic diversification for the country. The weight of the mining industry has significantly increased over the last decade, rising from 14% in 2010 to 17.7% in 2019. Sectoral analysis also shows that mining activities have become the main source of economic growth over the last four years. Since 2016, extractive industries have represented an average of 16.4% of GDP, compared to agriculture (7.7%) and services (6.6%). For the same period from 2016 to 2019, the sector represented an average of 45% of the value added in the secondary sector, thus driving the country's economic growth in recent years.*

• *Thanks to mining export revenues, the country's* ***foreign exchange reserves have stabilized****, leading to a stabilization of the exchange rate of the Guinean franc against major currencies. Between 2010 and 2019, exports more than doubled, increasing from about USD 1* *billion to USD 2.5 billion. This increase is particularly noticeable in 2017, the year in which mining exports exceeded 2.2 billion USD for the first time. The upward trend in exports makes Guinea one of the top five exporters in the West African subregion. According to data from the Central Bank of the Republic of Guinea (BCRG), the central bank's gross reserves increased from USD 498 million in 2015 to USD 1.44 billion as of June 30, 2021, tripling, mainly due to repatriation of foreign currency from mining.*

- *In terms of* ***induced impacts of the mining industry on other sectors*** *of the economy, the study showed that investments in the last four years have led to an increase in the value added of the construction sector by 4.04%, hospitality and catering services by 2.11%, real estate and business services by 2.49%, and financial services by 3.17%, to name just a few sub-sectors.*

The evaluation shows that these reforms have yielded encouraging results between 2011 and 2020, which deserve to be consolidated in the coming years. However, consultants have noted some challenges the sector must address, primarily:

- Strengthening local governance in the context of increased resources for local authorities;
- Identifying and promoting socio-economic investments to catalyze local development opportunities, especially basic socio-economic infrastructure;
- Ensuring that mining companies adhere to their community commitments, particularly environmental, for better coexistence with local communities;
- Enhancing the capacity of the mining administration in the context of international competition;

- Local transformation of mining production for more added value, particularly bauxite production;
- Promoting local content to maximize the impact of mining investments on the local economy.

9

Negotiations: a pragmatic patriotism

Mineral development often involves the conclusion of specific mining agreements. The Mining Code (and its implementing regulations) is the default mining agreement that applies to any mining project, covering the guarantees provided by the state, as well as the rights and obligations of various stakeholders.

This was the case for the Société Minière de Boké[13] (SMB, a Guinean-Sino-French-Singaporean consortium) for several years. Some questioned why this company did not have a specific mining agreement. In fact, the Mining Code served as the de facto mining agreement for this company. It is also not surprising that others wonder why mining companies often need specific mining agreements. This question, frequently asked, finds its initial answer in the Mining Code, which grants mining companies the right to request and obtain a specific mining agreement.

The granting of an agreement by the State does not necessarily mean that the mining company benefits from exemptions from the provisions of the Mining Code. For

[13] Founded in 2014, SMB is a joint venture between Singapore's Winning Shipping Ltd, China's Shandong Weiqiao, United Mining Supply, and the Guinean State.

the company, this primarily involves ensuring that the provisions provided for in the Mining Code, particularly those which are favorable to it, remain in force for the project for a certain period. Indeed, as I have already mentioned, for the investor, the period of return on investment could exceed ten years. In addition to his equity investment to be recovered, he might have borrowed funds from financial institutions to carry out the project. If the Mining Code in force is modified two or three years after the financing and construction of the project, and this increases, for example, the amount of taxes and royalties by 5 to 10 %, this could, by the discrepancy in comparison to the financial and economic assumptions of the project, lead to negative effects that could go so far as to make the company structurally loss-making, and thus, up to complete bankruptcy. It is to protect itself against this type of change and others with financial, legal, or commercial, direct or indirect impact, that the company legitimately seeks to stabilize the provisions of the Mining Code for its project. As in any financing, it is necessary to reduce or eliminate, if possible, all the risks of unpleasant surprises calling into question the basis on which the investment decision was taken.

Having a mining agreement is therefore an option, a right for a mining company, enshrined in the Mining Code. It is also a means of preserving the profitability of its project and protecting its investment in the event of possible changes to mining legislation.

The need for investment protection is not the only reason why investors request a mining agreement. This demand can also be related to the scale of the investment. The Mining Code pertains to the operation of the mine. However, in the case of certain projects, investments in infrastructure can be even more substantial than in mining works, installations, and equipment. This is particularly true for bulk minerals (iron, bauxite, etc.), where investments in infrastructure have often accounted for two-thirds of the total investment in projects in Guinea. In cases where investments in processing, transportation, or evacuation infrastructure become significantly more substantial than those in the mine itself, for a large-scale integrated project, discussions around a mining agreement and potential related agreements go far beyond simply adapting a mining agreement template. It involves a negotiation process that takes at least several months of intensive work.

The main challenge for a public administration with limited capacities is to negotiate on an equal footing with multinational corporations and their teams of lawyers and other advisers. The reform undertaken in the sector since 2011 has also addressed this aspect. As part of the review of mining agreements and permits initiated in 2012, a system was established that forms the basis of the negotiation framework now systematically adopted by the government. A Technical Committee for the Review of Mining Agreements and Permits (CTRCTM), overseen by a Strategic Committee (ministerial level), conducted the renegotiation of mining agreements with the support of a consortium of four of the world's top law firms. This process, already provided for and regulated by the 2011 Mining Code, was supported by technical and financial partners who, beyond funding law firms, also mobilized technical and financial experts that accompanied this process, now cited as an example, especially in the context of the Organization for Economic Cooperation and Development (OECD) dialogue on natural resource-based development[14]. At the end of the review process in April 2016, the Ministry of Mines continued negotiations on the same basis, within a framework that had already been tested and well understood by stakeholders at all levels.

Each negotiation involves the establishment of a negotiation committee that includes other relevant ministries. This committee is supported by one or more law firms, technical, and financial advisers. The role of the Strategic Committee is assumed by the Minister of Mines, the Minister of Budget (co-signatory of the agreements), as well as any other minister directly involved in the agreement under negotiation; for example, the Minister of Transportation for an agreement involving a railway. When the agreement is finalized and approved by the relevant ministers, it is transmitted to all members of the government as part of the submission to the Inter-ministerial Council (chaired by the Prime Minister), which reviews and subsequently submits it to the Council of Ministers (chaired by the Head of State). Only after this final step is the agreement signed by the ministers (Mines and Budget), submitted to parliament, and then to the constitutional court, before the signing of the decree promulgating the law that the agreement has become. This systematic process, which aims to inform, raise awareness, and obtain the agreement of all stakeholders, is now standard practice. While transparency through this consultation process is now the norm, it was not the case in the not-so-distant past in the Guinean mining sector. Far from it.

To pass the examination of this robust and crucial process, having the best advisory firms and well-equipped

---

[14] Guinea co-chairs with Germany the working group on "Getting better deals" in the OECD Policy Dialogue on Natural Resource-based Development (PD-NR). https://www.oecd.org/dev/natural-resources/getting-better-deals.htm

committees is not enough. It is necessary to ensure that the country's interests are preserved at every stage of the negotiation process leading to the agreement to be introduced into the formal process.

Regarding the process, it involves mastering the crucial question of information management during negotiations, both towards the other party and the press. Uncontrolled leaks can pose a risk to the Guinean state's position or even create a crisis of trust between the parties. A few years before my appointment as Minister of Mines, I experienced the extreme situation of the complete leakage of a major agreement that Guinea was negotiating, even before the lawyers had finished reviewing the document! The shock of this event, and others I witnessed, guided my commitment to ensuring secure information management during the negotiation process when I became Minister of Mines. However, transparency is essential once an agreement is obtained and validated[15].

It was not uncommon in the past for some members of negotiation teams, for one reason or another, to leak the content to sabotage the process. I drew the main lesson that bloated negotiation teams were dangerous for the integrity of the process, beyond their inefficiency. We often formed small, controlled teams, and when necessary (given the complexity of the case), cascading teams with small specialized/thematic subgroups. With a restricted and controlled scheme, we were able to conduct the most sensitive negotiations, sometimes over more than a year, without any leaks.

The integrity of the process, considering the defense of the state's interests, is also guaranteed by clear directives on negotiation positions known to all members of the

[15] Article 217-II of the Mining Code states that "All Mining Permits, as well as any Mining Agreement, are published in the Official Gazette".

small team in the case of less sensitive negotiations. In the case of highly sensitive negotiations, the basic principle has often been to share the actual negotiation positions only with the team leader, who is responsible for assigning each member the role to advance the negotiation strategy until the state's objective is achieved. Each member effectively plays their part without the ability to derail the process from the established line. With the support of lawyers and other advisors, and the involvement of other team members, no member can act unilaterally or alter the state's negotiation position. The systematic use of financial models reviewed by our advisors, incorporating all financial flows of the project in favor of each party, allows for negotiations that are as objective and quantitative as possible, leaving little room for unjustified positions. In terms of form, in addition to assuming all our administrative needs independently, the costs related to these negotiations are covered by the Ministry of Mines or charged to the project based on a formal agreement to avoid any means of pressure from the opposing party on the negotiation team.

Indeed, no precaution is excessive to preserve the integrity of the negotiation process. Knowing that some organizations are willing to deploy significant research or even espionage to gather information, it becomes clear that one is never entirely safe. During certain negotiations, despite our warnings, the opposing party recorded the entire discussions. This practice led us to always prefer negotiations on neutral ground, meaning in another country than that of the investor. Remaining in the other party's country served as a lesson to the director of a major international group who was inadvertently congratulated by the director of another group at the beginning of a meeting, just before which he had discreetly sealed a confidential agreement. Even in the case of a meeting on neutral ground, one is not immune to leaks. A mission I conducted in a Western city in secret did not stay secret for long, as someone much more in the know called to verify my presence at the hotel on my first day, without me being able to identify the person. Minimal precautions, therefore, involve never adopting imprudent habits and keeping any critical information for negotiation carefully guarded. However, it is worth noting that despite their extraordinary resources, large organizations are run by fallible human beings. Some may forget highly strategic notes on a worktable or simply discard them in a trash bin. Discovering such treasures has sometimes aided us in extremely challenging negotiations.

On the substantive side, each negotiation is unique, with three different dimensions. First, the ***context of the project***, namely its own economic and financial parameters. These parameters vary from one project to another and cannot be replicated identically. For example, two projects with the same purpose and size may have differences related to the nature of investors, the implementation site, processes, etc.

Secondly, there is the ***national context***, which can vary from one period to another. A project initiated in 2014 during the Ebola epidemic would require more facilities than the same project initiated in the post-Ebola period. The context can also be considered different between the period before and after the construction of significant public infrastructure in the area where the same project is implemented.

Finally, the ***international context*** prevailing at the time of the investment initiative (and its prospects) is crucial for the negotiation conditions. Gold projects might be negotiated under more favorable conditions for the state in

July 2020[16], with gold prices significantly higher than five years earlier.

These three sets of parameters (project-specific, national, and international) determine the flexibility of the negotiating positions of both the state and the investors. Without quantifying it, we assess the reasonableness and level of flexibility to adopt in each negotiation accordingly, based on the reference financial model. It is clear that the attitude of the investor on the other side always gives an idea of what we can adopt, without overlooking the role-playing in which both parties are experts.

The last key element in the negotiation process is the time available to the team to conclude. Generally, my belief is that one can achieve almost anything that is reasonable, and even more, for the state if time is not a constraint. Unfortunately… time is always a constraint. Even though it is becoming less of one over the years, especially in the bauxite industry, where we believed as early as 2018 that we had enough mature projects to seize opportunities in the international market.

Despite the importance of the time factor, showing that one is in a hurry always leads to missed opportunities for obtaining concessions, especially when facing negotiators as seasoned as those of mining companies. Bluffing is, therefore, more than useful to avoid this trap. I remember difficult negotiations with a large company that only relented when they understood that I was ready to forgo the agreement and catch the next flight. They still pushed the discussions to the end, catching up with me at the airport for the incongruous signing in the airport lounge, even though they had two weeks to do it! This investor has

---

[16] London Bullion Market Association (LBMA) Gold price went from US$ 1,068.32 in December 2015 to US$ 1,971.17 in August 2020. https://www.lbma.org.uk/prices-and-data/precious-metal-prices#/

already invested hundreds of millions of dollars in Guinea and started production on their project. It seems to suggest that they were probably more eager for that famous signature than we were.

The difficulty of a negotiation can sometimes be a sign of the seriousness that the investor attaches to their commitments or the investor's willingness to obtain conditions required by third parties (lenders, other investment partners, etc.). The teams of a major investor put us through extremely difficult days and nights, sometimes with altercations bordering on physical aggression due to the high tension. At the end of the negotiations, they congratulated the team members, expressing pride in seeing people passionately defend their country. In the end, they honored all the hard-won commitments that have already led to the production of the project after several hundred million dollars in investments.

Another challenging negotiation taught me that credible threats are sometimes the only recourse in extreme situations. A credible threat is a threat that is obviously serious in its potential impact, and you must have the capacity as well as the willingness to carry it out if the demand is not met. One evening in September 2016, I found myself facing the director of a large company who did not seem willing to yield to important requests for the country that we deemed reasonable. In addition to politely formulating my credible threat, I felt compelled to refer, in contradiction to my usual restraint, to the risk that his company faced of very regrettable consequences by using the metaphor "bloodshed" if our demand was not satisfied. I was in fact referring to the ultimate sanction for a mining company: the withdrawal of its mining title. I was forced to withdraw these inappropriate words in the face of the shock it caused my interlocutor. But the damage was done, with still positive consequences because my interlocutor took the threat seriously and eventually acceded to our request a few weeks later.

As paradoxical as it may seem, difficult and often lengthy negotiations mainly have the advantage of creating a negotiation team, consisting of representatives from both the state and the investor, who know each other well and have a perfect mastery of all project details. This has often facilitated the implementation of projects that representatives from both sides have fully embraced, becoming almost solid partners over the months.

While the difficulty of negotiations can be appreciated, they must always take place in an atmosphere of professional trust and respect. An extreme situation during a certain negotiation, especially in terms of verbal violence and falsification of points of agreement, led to enormous difficulties in the project's implementation, which could only move forward when the main protagonists were later removed.

Always being aware that any negotiation, regardless of its complexity or difficulty, is conducted by men and women is the most important lesson I have drawn from dozens of negotiations in the mines. These are individuals who may have weaknesses, feelings, fall ill, or simply become tired or crack under pressure. I have sometimes seen people yield because they were tired or unwell, or after spending too much time away from their families. I have also witnessed some psychologically break down and collapse because we had succeeded in exposing and dismantling their negotiation tactics.

Facing seasoned negotiators, Guinean teams have sometimes included individuals who cannot negotiate for more than two consecutive hours, and others who are eager to go shopping or return to sleep. Fortunately, the teams I had the chance to lead at the ministry were almost always composed of individuals demonstrating patriotism and high-level competence, with a will and determination that often impressed the opposing parties, who, nonetheless, had seen it all. The results obtained from negotiating over twenty agreements in five years were primarily due to their professionalism. And, above all, thanks to their patriotism, given the importance of the interests at stake, the human temptations they could have succumbed to, and the lack of scruples on the part of some opposing parties.

Negotiations can be triggered either by a spontaneous investment initiative from the title-holding company or as a direct consequence of the allocation of a deposit or a transfer to a new investor. Among the most emblematic examples are the iron ore deposits of Nimba and Blocks 1 and 2 of Simandou. These two deposits were awarded through competitive procedures, with one involving the transfer of shares by the main shareholder (EuroNimba) for Nimba and the other being an international tender conducted by the State for Blocks 1 and 2 of Simandou. The primary challenge for these deposits lies in the financing and construction of transport and evacuation infrastructure, as is the case for most large bulk ore deposits (especially bauxite and iron). Despite recurrent questions about the evacuation route for these deposits (Liberia or Guinea), the options chosen by the Guinean government are clear and objective. The iron ore deposits in the southeast of the country are categorized into three groups:

- Small-sized deposits located near the Liberian border (thus, very far from the Guinean coast), which have no chance of being profitable other than by evacuating the ore through the Liberian route. This includes the Zogota deposit, situated around 350 km from the Liberian coast and over 700 km from the Guinean coast.

- Large-sized deposits relatively close to the Guinean coast and profitable through evacuation from said coasts. The significant iron ore deposit of Simandou, located approximately 650 km from the Guinean coast and over 400 km from the Liberian coast, falls into this category. The feasibility study conducted by Rio Tinto in 2016 (solely on the blocks 3 and 4 deposit) confirmed that the project is not only profitable but could eventually become one of the most profitable iron ore projects globally.
- Finally, an intermediate category, in which the Nimba deposit is situated, approximately 300 km from the Liberian coast and over 700 km from the Guinean coast. The geographical location and the significant quantity of high-quality iron ore in this deposit do not allow for a determination of its viability. Therefore, the State has required that the choice of the evacuation route be based on the results of a feasibility study of the project's evacuation through the Guinean coasts. Authorization for evacuation through Liberia is only granted in the case of non-viability through the *Transguinean* route.

These options formed the basis of negotiations with the entities wishing to develop these deposits.

The Nimba deposit is a large deposit located in the Lola prefecture, which was majority owned by the EuroNimba joint venture (BHP, 43.5 %, NEWMONT, 43.5 % and ORANO, 13 %) up to 95 %. The project company, the Société des Mines de Fer du Nimba (SMFG), held an agreement (the development agreement) and a concession (the mining title) dating from 2003. Despite the negotiation of an agreement to transfer the shares of EuroNimba to a new buyer in 2013, following BHP and AREVA's wish to withdraw, the actual sale did not take place. After several months of selection between several candidates, EuroNimba finally submitted to the State, in March 2018, a potential buyer of all its shares in SMFG.

In such situations, the Ministry ensures, through a verification procedure, that the buyer has the skills and experience necessary to develop the proposed project while meeting the State's goals. Given the sensitive nature of the Nimba site (which houses the site, adjoining the mining site, listed as a World Heritage Site by UNESCO) and the importance of the deposit for the country, verifications and discussions took several months. Initially, we had to verify the quality of the acquirer, then negotiate with them a new agreement that would be an opportunity to address certain shortcomings of the old agreement. We were quickly reassured about the quality of HPX (a subsidiary of I-Pulse), a company belonging to the same mining group as Ivanoe Mines, with a worldwide reputation. The negotiations, which began in October 2018, after setting the negotiation principles on the main subjects of interest, culminated in the signing of the mining agreement on September 5, 2019. This negotiation enabled us, among other things, to improve state revenue shares, including (new) non-contributory shares of up to 15 %. Contrary to some claims, the state did not "sell" the Nimba. A private investor (HPX) took over the shares of other private investors (BHP, Newmont and Orano, formerly Areva) in the joint venture (EuroNimba), on the condition that the acquirer reimburse the seller what corresponded to historical costs (basically, expenses incurred to date).

As for the Simandou blocks 1 and 2 deposit[17], a tender launched in July 2019 resulted in a provisional award to the best bidder, the Winning Consortium SMB, in November 2019. This company was the one that formally

[17] The northern part of the Simandou mine, one of the largest undeveloped high-grade deposits in the world. The southern part (blocks 3 and 4) is controlled by Rio Tinto.

committed to building the *Transguinean railway*[18], a key objective of the State and a condition for the award. Negotiations with this company lasted a year and culminated in the signing of all agreements (mining, port, and railway).

In both cases (Nimba and Simandou Blocks 1 and 2), the State did not "sell" the deposits. The State, in any case, does not have the mandate to "sell" deposits. Instead, it grants concessions to companies that pay taxes and dividends while creating jobs and economic activities. In exceptional cases, the State may receive financial compensation, especially for deposits for which it holds valuable information (including studies) and/or assets that have been subject to investments. This was the case for Simandou blocks 1 and 2, for which the State obtained an amount that it had asked competing candidates to propose freely. This approach aimed to avoid the same failure as in the bauxite blocks of Boffa, where the State set entry amounts that no candidate proved able to pay, leading to the outright cancellation of the procedure, which became unsuccessful.

The primary objective of the State is the development and operation of mines. Therefore, if the payment of compensation before operation becomes an obstacle to investment in the project, the obvious choice is to prioritize operation, which can bring all the expected benefits (revenue, employment, local content, local development, etc.) for decades. The State, in its sovereign position, does not "sell" deposits; they always remain its property even as the asset depletes over the years of operation. It grants, for a certain period, exclusive exploitation rights to a company or consortium. At the end

---

[18] 650 km long railway project crossing the country to connect the iron ore mines of Simandou (south-eastern Guinea) with a proposed new port on the Atlantic coast at Forecariah (south of the capital Conakry).

of the concession period or upon cancellation of the concession, the State regains all its rights over the existing assets/resources or what remains of them, which were subject to the concession.

The negotiations of agreements rightly attract a lot of attention and discussion in Guinea and almost everywhere else. They involve significant commitments regarding, in the case of mines, valuable national resources. There are often difficult trade-offs to make, a constant tug-of-war between short-term urgencies and long-term imperatives. This also applies to the tension between the need for a profitable and viable project and the imperative to maximize benefits for the State. The most important thing is that the choices reconcile the inherent contradictions in any negotiation process, one that, conducted in a relative balance of power, inevitably leaves each of the two parties somewhat dissatisfied. One thing is certain: we used all our strength, all our experience and that of seasoned advisers, to obtain everything we can for the country. Did we get everything we wanted in the negotiations we conducted? Of course not. Did we do everything perfectly in the negotiations of the agreements we signed? Certainly not. If we had to start over, we might have improved some things at a different time and in a different context (regarding the project, the national and the international levels). That is the very nature of negotiations. However, considering the objective economic, technical, legal, and commercial constraints related to the context of each negotiation, we took positions that we believed were the best for Guinea at the time. We might have made different choices if the negotiations were conducted in an objectively different context (commercially, technically, economically, and legally) at another time. But for that, we would have needed a time machine or a crystal ball to predict the future. In any case, the commitments arising from these agreements bind Guinea and the investors. Each party must fully assume them. Each party has the responsibility, the duty, to ensure their proper implementation by all their representatives. However imperfect they may be for the State, on the one hand, and for the investor and lenders, on the other. So that perfection is not the enemy of the good. So that the country progresses.

10

The issue of mining revenues

The effectiveness of granting special tax benefits in attracting investment in relation to their cost is a subject of debate. It is challenging to distinguish between those who advocate for the positions of their interest groups and those who, in a neutral approach, genuinely defend positions they consider objective. Seeking the truth in the intricacies of justifications and impacts of tax incentives is therefore a daunting task. So many objective and subjective factors contribute to encouraging an investor to make the decision to take the plunge. Not to mention the numerous uncertain assumptions underlying the investor's primary motivation: projected profitability. The debate on tax incentives will certainly never be closed. Some argue that improving other aspects of the investment framework (legal and regulatory framework, infrastructure, bureaucracy, corruption, etc.) should be the lever for attracting investments, suggesting avoiding the easy but deemed ineffective solution of tax incentives in order not to avoid the challenging reforms of the investment framework. Others support a realistic approach, emphasizing the time reforms take in underdeveloped countries that urgently need investment. Some also argue that globalization, the reduction of tariff barriers, exchange liberalization, and the strong internationalization of multinational companies are factors that make tax incentives more relevant than they have been in the past.

Without delving into the age-old debate on the effectiveness of tax incentives, it is important to analyze their relevance in the context of the Guinean mining industry without bias. Some consider tax incentives inappropriate or ineffective for a country like Guinea based on their analysis of study results, which, even if serious, cannot be systematically applied to all countries. They assert or imply that Guinea does not need tax incentives to attract investment, for example, based on a UNIDO survey of 7,000 companies in 19 countries in 2011[19]. While not questioning the credibility of this survey, it is important to avoid, as is often the case, extrapolating from an international survey what its results cannot imply for Guinea in particular. This survey concludes that tax incentives rank only 11th out of 12 factors motivating decisions on the choice of an investment location.

What the survey does not say, and should not be made to say, is that Guinea's direct competitors, whether developed or emerging countries, outperform our country on the majority (if not all) of the top 10 factors. This makes the 11th factor (tax incentives) de facto much more determinant than it appears in a general context. Moreover, unlike tax incentives, the top 10 factors take more time to change in practice and especially in the perception of investors. These include economic and political stability, access to raw materials, legal framework, business environment, market size, quality of

---

[19] UNIDO (2012), Africa Investor Report 2011: Towards Evidence-based Investment Promotion Strategies, UNIDO, Vienna, https://www.unido.org/sites/default/files/2013-02/AIS_Report_A4_0.PDF

infrastructure, presence of skilled workforce, and the cost of labor or quality of life in the country.

Even though deposits are not relocatable, mining companies have the option to invest in Guinea or another country, if they can find the ore with the desired characteristics (which is presumably the case for all known substances in Guinea). Beyond qualitative factors, the factual observation is that incentives serve as a means for Guinea to address the economic and financial competitiveness gap, or rather profitability, of projects in the country compared to comparable projects in other countries.

Despite the continuous improvement in Guinea's attractiveness over the last decade, the country faces at least two handicaps in this area that justify, at least until now, tax concessions to attract certain investments in the mining sector. First, the inadequacy of infrastructure forces mining investors to allocate a larger share of their resources to infrastructure compared to countries with more developed infrastructure. Second, the greater distance between Guinea and the largest market, China, creates an unfavorable gap in transport costs for our country. On these two points, some countries like Australia, a major competitor in bauxite and iron, have a head start over Guinea. For example, a bauxite project can save up to two-thirds of the investment if it is carried out in a country that already has a railway and a port, compared to a country that does not. Moreover, the transport cost per tonne of bauxite from Guinea to China can easily exceed $20 US dollars (it has reached peaks since the Covid-19 pandemic), while Australia's cost for the same destination is generally below $10 US dollars. All other things equal, Guinea has a handicap to overcome on each project to compensate for these gaps in freight and infrastructure investment. This necessarily implies tax concessions to make projects competitive in terms of profitability.

The issue of mining revenues, in relation to tax concessions, raises concerns due to several inaccurate analyses that are often made, including by some who sincerely care about the outcomes of mining activities. These analyses create confusion, resulting in a biased view of the progress made in recent years and a diversion of attention from significant challenges.

The first inaccurate analysis concerns the objectivity and legal basis for granting tax exemptions. These exemptions are never ad hoc in the mining industry but follow a negotiation process that leads to the signing of agreements that include these exemptions. They are now granted in an objective approach based on a financial model that takes into account the investment needs in infrastructure, especially for bulk minerals such as bauxite and iron. The involvement of the Ministry of Mines upstream, through the fiscal clauses of mining agreements, is done under the supervision of the Ministry of Budget. In all cases, the agreements are submitted to the National Assembly, which adopts them before they come into effect. The twenty or so agreements that I had the opportunity to present to parliament were adopted, along with their fiscal clauses, by the favorable vote of all deputies, representing various political affiliations, with only one abstention during the vote on two agreements.

Furthermore, the application of the hierarchy of norms (laws) confirms the validity of an ordinary law (thus of the same level as the Mining Code) passed under the same conditions (absolute majority of deputies in the National Assembly) in a specific area. Only provisions contrary to an organic law (that requires a qualified majority meaning a reinforced majority) or the Constitution can challenge those of a particular agreement validly established as an ordinary law. To my knowledge, there is nothing of the sort. The same applies to the exceptions voted on each year in the budget law in derogation of existing codes. To accommodate the need to attract investment and generate revenue for the state over time, agreements generally provide for the application of the mining tax and income tax at the end of a certain tax holiday period, as well as dividends related to the non-contributory state participation.

In summary, the Ministry of Mines does not unilaterally and secretly determine the level of taxes and fees. The Ministry of Mines does not collect taxes and fees. It does not allocate the amounts collected within the framework of the programming and budgeting process. It also does not execute the expenses of the national budget. However, many regularly raise questions with the Ministry of Mines regarding the issue of mining revenues. Exemptions are a collective decision of the Guinean state. They are neither the decision of a single ministry nor of the executive alone, but rather that of the entire Guinean state, including the parliament composed of elected representatives of the people, including those from the opposition.

The legitimate question that arises is the basis upon which the level of exemption is determined. In practice, each concession is granted based on its impact on the profitability of the project, which is determined through a financial model and its cost to the state. This model takes into account all financial flows entering or leaving the project for the benefit of stakeholders (particularly the investor and the state) over the project's lifespan.

Typically, the investor submits a financial model that encompasses all financial flows of the project. The model is audited by the state's financial advisors, based on their knowledge of similar-profile projects and market conditions, to ensure the accuracy, relevance, and completeness of the financial information. Negotiations are then conducted with the investor to achieve a reasonable level of project profitability (neither negative nor excessively positive) in comparison to similar projects' profitability levels and in line with the state's objectives, particularly regarding the preservation of the most secure sources of revenue for Guinea (specifically the mining tax).

In the context of negotiations with Guinea's technical and financial partners, beyond quantitative estimates based on financial models and to address the realities of investment in Guinea's mines, the relevance of exemptions was confirmed in June 2018 under the International Monetary Fund's (IMF) Extended Credit Facility (ECF) for mining projects involving shared infrastructure and/or local processing units[20].

Being concerned about tax exemptions is legitimate. However, it is also legitimate to first address the level of tax collection to which companies are already subject, as well as the rational use of the collected revenues. It is indeed more relevant and fairer to ensure effective collection and efficient use of revenues before considering increasing the tax burden on companies. Otherwise, there is a risk that raising the level of taxation may have the negative effects (on the incentive to invest) inherent in such an initiative without realizing the expected benefits (on income levels and the quality of expenditures).

Mining, like most sectors involving large international companies (telecoms, financial sector, infrastructure, and logistics, etc.), is one of the sectors with a high risk of tax evasion, including in developed countries. Countries face the risk of tax evasion through transfer pricing, through

---

[20] International Monetary Fund. 2018. IMF Country Report No. 18/234, P.12. Washington, DC: International Monetary Fund.

the overvaluation of expenses or the undervaluation of the revenues of subsidiaries in favor of other companies in the group, thus excluding taxable profits from income and dividends tax. It is therefore essential that efforts continue for the effectiveness of the identification and collection of taxes and fees so that the state can truly assess the impact of tax exemptions in mining and beyond.

Strengthening tax control, without it turning into harassment, of companies in all relevant fields (to avoid stigmatizing the mining companies, which are not the only ones concerned) could be a good start. Despite its weight in the economy, mining should not be subject to stigmatization harmful to investment in an industry that represents on average more than 90% of private investments in recent years.

The second inaccurate analysis concerns the evolution of revenues. There is sometimes a tendency to say that mining revenues are decreasing when, in reality, they are increasing. This is often a misuse of language to convey that mining revenues realized in a given year fall short of the budgetary projections for that same year, which would correspond to a 'shortfall' in forecasts rather than a 'decrease.' In other words, it means not achieving the revenue projections for the year and not a decrease compared to the previous year. In practice, direct mining revenues recorded in public accounts increased from 115 million US dollars in 2010 to 397 million US dollars in 2019[21], representing a 245% increase over this period!

---

[21] MNH Consulting, Impact study of the mining sector on the national economy ("Etude d'impact du secteur minier sur l'économie nationale"). 2020. p.31-32. https://www.itie-guinee.org/guinee-limpact-des-reformes-du-secteur-minier-durant-les-dix-dernieres-annees/
https://www.cabinetetudesmnh.com/

However, this evolution does not account for the revenues generated by mining subcontractors whose contracts exist solely because of mining operations. Considering these purchases from subcontractors, including local purchases that averaged the equivalent of 90 million US dollars per year over the last decade, would certainly show a more significant impact of the mining industry on state revenues. The evolution of direct revenues generated by the entire sector for all public stakeholders demonstrates a significant growth in income. Indeed, reports from the Extractive Industries Transparency Initiative (EITI), based on independent assessments, show that overall revenues generated by the extractive sector nearly doubled between 2015 and 2018, rising from 293 million US dollars to 544 million US dollars (including over 60 million US dollars paid by mining subcontractors)[22].

At times, some adopt an inaccurate approach to the point of comparing the amounts paid to the state per tonne by the Compagnie des Bauxites de Guinée (CBG)[23] and those paid by other companies operating under the current Mining Code. For example, comparing the amount of $10 per tonne paid by CBG until recently to the $3 per tonne paid by companies newly operating under the Mining Code is approximate, if not inaccurate. This confusion is fueled by some actors applying a simple proportionality, stating that if one tonne from CBG generates $10 in revenue for the state, then one tonne from any other company should also generate $10.

---

[22] EITI Guinea. 2015 and 2018 Reports. https://www.itie-guinee.org/rapport-2018/; https://www.itie-guinee.org/rapport-2015/

[23] CBG is owned by Halco Mining Inc. (51%) and the Guinean State (49%). Halco is a consortium comprised of Rio Tinto, Alcoa and Dadco Investments. CBG holds the largest bauxite reserves of Guinea. Founded in 1963, it started its bauxite operations in 1973.

However, the amounts paid by CBG are equivalent to the taxes, fees, and dividends paid by a company that has been in existence for over half a century, with long-amortized investments. Regarding dividends, it should be noted that the state owns 49% of the shares in this company. Some might argue that the state should have 49% of new companies to receive more revenue, but that would require revising the Mining Code, which caps the state's non-contributory shares at 15% (also improperly called "free shares," which they are not, as they are the counterpart of the provision of national resources). This level of participation was achieved through consultations that resulted in a Mining Code that is evidently attractive for investment in a country that was sorely lacking it in mining.

Contrary to some assumptions, the industrial process of CBG is not the main factor behind the significant difference between its payment level and that of new companies. In comparing the payments made by CBG with those of other new companies, it is also important not to forget that, unlike the new companies that self-finance their infrastructure, the CBG's railway was built with a loan of $100 million (equivalent to approximately $800 million today) obtained by the Guinean government in the mid-1960s. The government only finished repaying this amount in 1992.

Should the government incur debt today in the hundreds of millions to finance commercial infrastructure that private entities are willing to fund, instead of allocating these resources to basic socioeconomic infrastructure? The answer seems evident to me.

Beyond the investment conditions of that time in a less capitalist world, investing in infrastructure probably entitled the state to have these 49% of shares in the company. Moreover, even if the state had 49% of newly established companies, it would not have received significant dividends or profits taxes during the very first years of these companies' operation. These companies, like any new commercial operation, generally make little or no profit in the initial years, corresponding to the period of investment amortization and ramp-up. Even in the scenario where the state has 49% ownership, it would essentially rely on the mining tax (which is precisely around $3 US per tonne) in the early stages of production.

It is not surprising, then, that the recent investments by CBG in a capacity expansion project led to a reduction in the state's revenue due to the expenses related to investment amortization and loan repayment. In summary, while CBG pays what amounts to taxes (on profits), mining taxes, and dividends to Guinea, new mining companies essentially only pay the mining tax during these early years.

This situation is expected to evolve over the years through a gradual increase in payments from these new companies, which, in addition to mining taxes, should pay more and more dividends and profits taxes, gradually approaching the amounts paid by CBG per tonne. In the long run, the level of taxes and fees per tonne from these companies would only reach that of CBG if the level of state participation in these companies is equal to the 49% in CBG, all else being equal.

To avoid any misinterpretation of my remarks and analyses, I would like to emphasize that the statements and analyzes above do not in any way mean that I believed that the old or new mining companies did not undertake any action of tax evasion or avoidance, and that the new mining companies generate no tax on profits or dividends. My analyzes are based on the economic and financial profile of projects and companies, as well as the usual observations of the evolution of this profile during the very first years of activity. They are not and should not be interpreted as the result of an audit of the companies' accounts. In any case, the amounts of taxes recognized as real/accurate by the state can only be definitively established through a rigorous and proper tax audit.

The last approximate, even erroneous, analysis on mining revenues concerns the comparison of Guinea with other countries based on the percentage of GDP represented by mining revenues. On this front as well, it is crucial to be very cautious not to draw hasty conclusions. Two countries with the same mining operations may have a different proportion of mining revenues simply because the industry is not equally mature in both countries. Guinea's period of strong growth in mining activity barely covers five years. Can we compare the financial contribution of this mining industry to that of a country with established operations spanning several decades, featuring completely amortized investments and different levels of participation in the capital of mining companies?

Comparing countries must also be done with great caution, considering the difference in the types of substances produced in these countries. The financial contribution of a country's mining primarily producing gold (which requires fewer infrastructures) cannot be always comparable to that of a country primarily producing bulk minerals (such as bauxite and iron), where two-thirds of investments are in transport and evacuation infrastructure. In any case, any comparison of Guinea to other countries, or even Guinea at different times, that does not consider important variables (maturity of operations, production mix, level of infrastructure, recovery level, etc.) that determine the level of financial contribution, is incomplete, if not incorrect.

The negotiations conducted by Guinea with mining investors are certainly not perfect. However, thanks to continuously strengthening capabilities over several years and enhanced rigor in the approach, the country achieves results that deserve to be objectively appreciated. For example, in the negotiations on Blocks 1 and 2 of Simandou, the assessment by one of the largest international firms in the field showed that Guinea obtained better results than countries in the sub-region with comparable projects. In the evaluation of revenue distribution, these states obtained between 18.5% and 39.9% (with an average of 30.2%), compared to 45% for Guinea in the Simandou project (Blocks 1 and 2)[24].

It must nevertheless be recognized that, despite the growth in mining revenues, their level is still insufficient considering the country's needs and ambitions. These revenues should certainly increase with more efficiency in their collection, which is evidently not at full potential based on current regulations (Mining Code and agreements). Furthermore, unless there is a crisis (national or international) with a major impact on the mining industry, the level of state revenues is expected to inevitably grow over at least a decade as operations reach their cruising speed and exemptions come to an end. This increasing level of direct and immediate state revenues is an important factor in the contribution of mines to the country's development. The same applies to the use of potential and future state revenues as a lever for financing infrastructure. This is already the case with the Sino-Guinean framework agreement, which is backed by future revenues. The same approach could be taken for public-private partnerships in commercial or partially commercial projects in market-oriented areas. Finally, following the example of other countries, especially those with strong and viable mining, oil, or gas activities, the creation of a

[24] Ernst & Young Report. Benchmark on the distribution of project income. Ernst & Young. 2020.

sovereign wealth fund could be a turning point in using mining revenues as a powerful lever for the development of infrastructure and local industry. The need for governance ensuring the trust of all partners involved in the establishment and operationalization of such a fund requires absolute rigor in its structure, organization, and autonomous operation. The sovereign wealth fund would exclusively fund priority projects (based on financial, economic, and social impact) for the development of human capital and socio-economic infrastructure necessary for Guinea's emergence.

11

Geological research: a strategic, economic, and environmental requirement

Guinea, with its reputation as a 'geological scandal,' has an exceptional potential in terms of quality, quantity, and diversity of its mineral resources. The country holds the world's largest bauxite reserves, estimated at 40 billion tonnes, with a significant portion being high in alumina content, low in silica, and nearly at the surface. These characteristics make Guinean bauxite relatively easy to exploit and less expensive to transform into alumina. In addition to bauxite, Guinea has 20 billion tonnes of very high-quality iron ore (over 60% iron content), including the world's largest untapped high-grade iron deposit (Simandou) with an average content of 65%.

With an estimated potential of 700 tonnes of gold, mainly in the northeast of the country, Guinea has industrial operations that fall far short of the quality and extent of its deposits. While Mansa Musa, Emperor of Mali in the early 14th century, reputedly the richest person of all time, is said to have derived his wealth from the gold of Bouré, in the present-day prefecture of Siguiri, Guinea is the least industrially exploited gold-rich country in the region.

Diamonds (estimated reserves of 30 million carats), limestone (40 million tonnes), uranium, base metals (75 million tonnes) such as copper, lead, zinc, cobalt, manganese, and nickel, as well as black sand (zircon, rutile, ilmenite), complement this unique potential, which also includes graphite and rare earth elements.

In addition to traditional heavy industries such as aluminum and steel, the variety of substances present in Guinea allows the country to play a role in emerging industries such as information technology, batteries, solar panels, etc.

Despite this exceptional potential, only four substances are exploited in Guinea: bauxite, iron, gold, and diamond. Moreover, iron is still in its early stages with the gradual entry into production of the Forécariah mine[25]. This paradox is explained not only by the difficulty related to the business environment, which was long inappropriate for attracting massive investments for the exploitation of other substances but also by the insufficient geological information to ensure effective promotion of investment in the sector while reducing the risk for the investor. Therefore, mineral exploration needed to be intensified and accelerated to overcome this handicap, which also limits the government's capacity to rationalize mining by confining it only to potentially rich areas, thus substantially reducing the impact zones of mining activity.

Several research projects were conducted before and after independence, without providing the country with the necessary information to achieve the sustainable development goals of the sector. Between 1960 and 2007, five main research projects were implemented, of which only one, initiated in 1979, covered the entire territory. The first focused on creating a geological map on a scale

---

[25] Forecariah is located 100 km south of Conakry, on the Atlantic coast.

of 1/200,000 by the Russians, covering most of the country during the 1960s-1970s. In 2016, a comprehensive geological report, including geological and mineralogical maps, was produced by Mr. Mamedov of Geoprospects Ltd, published by Moscow State University (Russia).

Starting in 2016, we initiated an effective revival of research funding. The Mining Investment Fund, for which research funding is one of the main objectives, had so far provided little support for research. This needed to change. The most comprehensive project in terms of territorial coverage was the one focused on geophysical surveys and the creation of a geospatial database at 1/100,000 scale across the entire national territory. This project, initiated in 1979 by the First Republic, had not been completed more than thirty years later! Moreover, initially entrusted to the German company Geosurvey Gmbh, it had undergone many twists and turns before finally being assigned to the British company AMTEC from 2004. Like an urban legend, everyone had their story about the AMTEC project, making it extremely difficult to separate fact from fiction. It took me several months to understand that it was not a fictitious project and that the country indeed needed it. Once convinced, thanks to the insight of ministry officials and the three decades of perseverance of Mr. Thierno Souleymane Diallo (the project manager, may his soul rest in peace), I called for a reassessment of the two ongoing contracts for the project and their merger into a new single contract, which I was to sign with the Minister of Finance on January 18, 2017.

The completion of this project, entirely funded by the state through the Ministry of Mines, has provided Guinea with a digital geospatial database interpreted at a scale of 1/100,000 and geo-scientific data to identify potentially mineralized anomaly zones. This enables the deepening of research programs on base metals (nickel, chrome, cobalt, lithium, copper, lead, zinc, tin, rare earths, etc.) and the development of the country's mineral resources. For mining development, this then allowed investors to access new geo-scientific data (geophysical, geological, mineralogical, etc.) on their permit areas, enabling them to delineate research and exploration zones, thus reducing costs and search times. Beyond mining, the creation of an updated geospatial database covering the entire Guinean national territory accelerates development projects in eleven sectors, including operational land planning, agricultural activity development, road infrastructure management and development, tourism organization and development, watershed management, urbanization, etc.

The so-called “AMTEC” project allowed us to make significant but insufficient progress. We therefore opened several fronts in geological research.

Firstly, the revival of internal research in geophysical exploration and prospecting on a 1/25,000 scale in the northeastern region of the country. The pilot project, implemented between 2018 and 2020, covering an area of 500 km2 and costing approximately one million US dollars for the ministry, allowed ministry officials to be back in the field (with external technical assistance) in a research project implemented by the ministry for the first time in over two decades. To this end, state-of-the-art equipment was acquired for the intervention team, which was trained with the aim of enabling the implementation of such research projects entirely by Guinean staff moving forward.

Secondly, in addition to the resources mobilized by the ministry, assistance from technical and financial partners was obtained to hire a specialized firm for research. In this context, the support of the World Bank enabled us to implement, between 2018 and 2019, the geochemical survey project in stream sediments in the central-southern part of Guinea, with the main target being base metals (nickel, cobalt, chrome, lithium, manganese, etc.) and rare earths. This project, which also cost one million US dollars, covered an area of over 26,400 km2 in the prefectures of Kissidougou, Kérouané, and Guéckédou (central-southern region of Guinea).

The data and information from these various research projects have long been scattered among public and private entities, both local and foreign. That is why the government created, in 2018, the Geological Mapping and Information Center within the Ministry of Mines, to collect, centralize, and manage all the geo-scientific data and information in the country.

All these initiatives, along with others of lesser magnitude, have revitalized and better organized geological research in the sector, with the aim of significantly improving the geological knowledge of the country. This is to plan the exploitation of strictly prospective areas for a rational and sustainable environmental management, for the diversification of mining and economic activities, and for greater efficiency in promoting investment.

Despite the progress made, there is still a long way to go in terms of mobilizing financial resources and strengthening technical capacities to achieve a satisfactory level of geological knowledge. To bridge the capacity gap (financial and technical) of the state, the option has now been taken to encourage the conclusion of 'regional exploration' agreements with mining companies. These agreements, which cover a vast exploration area, provide for the state to receive back half of the discovered prospective perimeters. The first agreement implemented in this framework was signed in December 2019. It covers the central-southern region of the country (Kérouané,

Kissidougou, and Guéckédou) and should yield results in the near future.

In addition to geological research projects, strengthening the system for collecting and processing research results from companies on the permits they hold and improving the analysis capabilities of geological laboratories are initiatives whose effective implementation will ensure a substantial improvement in geological knowledge. After the renovation and equipping of the National Geology Laboratory in Conakry, mainly dedicated to bauxite and iron, we initiated the Kankan laboratory project (North-East of Guinea), which focuses primarily on gold and base metals. The goal is to make it one of the best, if not the best, reference laboratory for gold in the region.

The limited knowledge of subsurface resources means that for decades, non-prospective areas for mining operations have been covered by mining permits. This situation deprives the country of opportunities to develop other economic activities in these areas (tourism, agriculture, etc.) and poses a higher environmental risk. It also entails a higher level of risk for investors, who often have a small proportion of their perimeters that are exploitable.

Geological research is therefore a global issue, well beyond the economic challenge of attracting investment. It is a fundamental issue in diversifying economic development to ensure the goal of gradually reducing dependence on mining by releasing non-prospective areas for mining in favor of other development sectors. It is, finally, an environmental issue related to reducing the footprint of mining activities by confining them only to areas rich in mineral substances. All of this calls for the need to intensify funding for research activities, approaching them with a comprehensive perspective on national economic development.

12

Unprecedented investments in a more favorable framework

Guinea's mining industry, having recently emerged from the Ebola crisis, presented a crucial objective: attracting foreign direct investments. Fortunately, the reforms initiated during the epidemic laid the groundwork for progress. The mining industry's takeoff had long suffered from governance shortcomings that undermined investor confidence. The ongoing reform momentum provided a fertile ground for investment, a solid foundation for massive investments. However, it was essential to avoid missing opportunities for a mining boom, as had happened in the past due to a lack of understanding of the issues and a somewhat naive form of nationalism within the administration, believing that Guinea had the world's best deposits and, therefore, did not need to court investors. The approach required sincere but pragmatic patriotism in defending national interests rather than an insular form of nationalism.

I decided to adopt the most pragmatic approach possible by seizing all immediate opportunities that aligned with the short, medium, and long-term objectives of the existing mining policy. The goal was to achieve the maximum while avoiding the perfect becoming the enemy of the good. It was crucial to ensure that the constant pursuit of megaprojects did not come at the expense of smaller, more manageable projects that, collectively, could already constitute the equivalent of one or more megaprojects. In this pragmatic approach, small companies, commonly referred to as "juniors," were almost as important to us as the larger ones. We fully engaged in every project as long as the credibility, capabilities, and commitment of the company to execute the proposed project, along with the project's quality, were established.

Despite the urgency, I chose to take my time on the actual promotion of the sector. The reforms were underway, but several important ones were still unfinished. As long as reforms are ongoing, they create a certain uncertainty for investors. In such a configuration, some, the optimists, often decide to wait for the best conditions offered by the results of the reforms. Others, the pessimists, decide to wait for worse conditions to be established before claiming the restoration or confirmation of their previous rights before investing.

So, I simply made it clear to the team that we needed to focus first on completing the reforms. "You can't sell a house that isn't completely clean," I would tell them to justify limiting my promotional trips abroad to the bare minimum during the first few months. We also needed to improve the management of investors already present in the sector because they are the most credible promoters or advocates. One team member was exclusively responsible for this task, which took up most of his first year by my side. And no investor should be neglected, especially not the smaller ones. If we could satisfy the small investors, we would not have problems with the big investors, who have the resources and networks needed to navigate better. One of my greatest satisfactions in the efforts to build investor confidence concerns an American who could barely afford to invest $5 million. The first time I saw him, in early 2016, he was on the verge of a nervous breakdown with insurmountable difficulties across the chain of his operations at several state agencies. He had almost decided to leave Guinea. I asked a collaborator to follow him day by day, emphasizing that we absolutely had to make him stay and thrive for the sector to succeed. In my eyes, we had to treat this situation almost like a life-or-death matter for the country's mines. Through daily monitoring and unwavering support, we managed to save his project after a few months. Four years later, his company had two new projects in Guinea and decided to invest in sectors outside of mining! This investor became one of the strongest advocates for the Guinean mining sector and the government's reforms to improve the overall business climate.

At the end of the first semester of 2016, the main reforms were completed, and we had better material to travel the world to present the progress of the country's mines, being confident that investors could immediately benefit from these advances. Already, our participation in the Cape Town Indaba mining conference was receiving special attention from investors and other players. The plenary hall, which hosts successive presentations by countries, had eyes only for Guinea. The minister of a country in East Africa, who followed Guinea in the order of presentations, had the unpleasant surprise of finding himself in a room completely deserted by spectators, who had all decided to follow the Guinean delegation. Like bees swarming to a hive, my colleagues and I were inundated from all sides. All the solicitations only made us prouder of the momentum underway in the sector. Hope was allowed. But there was still a long way to go. To get there, we had to choose priorities.

Guinea has only commercially exported four substances over the long term: diamond, gold, bauxite, and alumina. Iron is only just beginning with Forécariah. Diversification was already a priority outlined in the country's mining policy. While working on diversification, it was necessary to maximize the potential of the minerals currently being exploited. The country's potential and two recent events clearly indicated that there should be a focus on bauxite: the recent start of production by the Société Minière de Boké (SMB), which had a unique setup and operating model in the industry, and the fact that Indonesia had banned the export of raw bauxite in 2014.

From my initial meetings with representatives of the Société Minière de Boké (SMB), I understood the significance of the seemingly risky choice they made to invest in Guinea without securing a quality deposit from the government with bauxite resources ensuring the viability of their operation. I understood the company was seeking profit opportunities. However, in line with traditional financial requirements, companies always demand access to a deposit whose exploitation guarantees a return on investment before committing equity or borrowed funds. The consortium was formed by the end consumer and land and sea logistics companies, together forming a complete chain of interests, ensuring the market outlet while having the greatest strategic and financial motivation to produce the maximum amount of bauxite. This was confirmed by the commitments, in terms of production quantity, that the company was ready to achieve in just three years. I did not take their word for it on this program, which seemed probably too ambitious to me. So, I demanded that they put their commitments in writing to avoid any freezing of the deposit, as often happens in the mines. This was done. And each year, their production grew exponentially to be around 35 million tonnes at the end of the third year. The company took two unprecedented options in the sector for significant investments. It invested before seeking access to mineral resources guaranteeing the return on investment. It chose to operate without a mining agreement, thus opting for the full application of the provisions of the Mining Code. This obviously allowed them to avoid long months of negotiations that would have cost them market opportunities. A mining agreement was only negotiated and signed at the time of the commitment to build the railway and refinery, a few years later.

At the same time, we continued aggressive promotion of investment in the mines. The development of existing projects also accelerated over the months. Guinea thus became the leading exporter of bauxite to China, reaching 60, 70, and then 80 million tonnes of production per year, with the goal of reaching 100 million tonnes.

Investors interested in Guinea realized that, in addition to having the world's best bauxite, the country was more welcoming to investors who could all expect more careful, transparent, and predictable handling of their cases, with goodwill at all levels, including the highest authorities in the country, if they were ready to act quickly and efficiently in compliance with regulations.

The window of opportunity presented by Indonesia's withdrawal from the market of raw bauxite (in 2014) is not the only explanation for the acceleration of mining development in Guinea. While this withdrawal did provide an opportunity to export, especially to China, to replace the exports from that country at the time of its export ban decision, how many similar opportunities did Guinea have before without being able to seize them? Several, with the most significant one in recent history being the great Chinese economic boom, during which China experienced double-digit growth rates from the early 1960s to the late

2000s. During this period, Chinese growth was above 10%, except for a few rare years (notably during the 2008 crisis). Despite the decline in growth in the 2010s (below 10%), Guinea still benefited from the Chinese market's appetite. The sustained acceleration over time is more explained by investor confidence than by a merely conjunctural situation. Otherwise, the momentum would have quickly faded once the investor community realized that the shining image presented by the Guinea's mines was just a mirage. It would have stopped after Indonesia's return to the market a few years later. This was not the case. Quite the contrary happened.

While the bauxite industry was taking off, we exerted all necessary efforts to propel the gold sector into the same momentum. The team devoted significant efforts to promotional activities, with some members dedicating most of their time to the gold sector that is primarily concentrated in the eastern part of the country. While ensuring the viability of existing operations with new investments (AngloGold's SAG in Siguiri, Nordgold's SMD in Dinguiraye), the entire team worked tirelessly to revive the Tri-K project (Mandiana), taken over by Managem (Morocco), and the Kiniéro project (acquired by Sycamore). A frustrating observation had to change: Guinea, situated in the vast Birimian basin (alongside Mali, Burkina Faso, Ghana, and Côte d'Ivoire), was the only country with only two active industrial gold mines and no immediate prospect of having several more. We adopted a systematic approach, identifying all credible companies in the global gold mining industry and engaging in a one-on-one approach with each of them. Companies like IamGold, BarrickGold, Newmont, etc., were all approached at one point or another to attract them to Guinea. At the very least, we did everything possible to make the best impression on them. The head of one of these companies, currently present in Guinea, later reported that they decided to invest in Guinea despite a terrible experience in the country in the past simply because Guinea's aggressive marketing approach seemed enticing and unusual with African mining countries.

After the bauxite boom, the upcoming years are likely to be those of gold, following the maturation of projects initiated in recent years. The industrial gold mining sector, like the entire mining sector, has benefited from the impact of reforms carried out since 2011. In addition, the quality of value and the safe-haven status that gold represents in times of crisis (such as the Covid-19 pandemic) have increased the price of gold by 25% between December 2019 and December 2020, rising from USD 1,480.03 to USD 1,853.80[26].

Beyond the positive effect of the rise in gold prices, the gold mining is attracting increasing interest in Guinea due to the perception among the investor community of low security risks in the medium and long term compared to other gold-producing countries in the region facing unfortunate security challenges. In this context, Guinea has an opportunity to increase industrial production, currently managed by only two companies.

Based on ongoing projects involving some major players, Guinea could bring several industrial mining operations into production in the coming years:

1. The project of the Société des Mines de Mandiana (SMM), a subsidiary of the Moroccan group Managem, with an investment of over $200 million and an expected annual production of 120,000 ounces starting from June 2021 in the Mandiana prefecture.

2. The ongoing revitalization project of the former Kiniéro mine in Kouroussa by the British company

---

[26] London Bullion Market Association (LBMA) Gold price. https://www.lbma.org.uk/prices-and-data/precious-metal-prices#/

Sycamore in the Kouroussa prefecture, with a planned investment of $176.2 million, foreseeing production of 42,000 ounces per year from 2022, followed by 70,000 and 120,000 ounces in subsequent phases.

3. The project by the British company Hummingbird Resources Plc in Kouroussa, which entails a $102 million investment for the revitalization of the Cassidy mine, targeting a production of 40,000 ounces per year starting from 2023.

4. The project by the Canadian company IamGold (with operational gold mines in Canada, Suriname, Mali, and Burkina Faso) that holds a deposit with the potential for industrial exploitation in the Mali prefecture, with a possibility of entering production within five to seven years, subject to a positive feasibility study.

5. The project by Endeavour, which is also in an advanced exploration phase in the Siguiri prefecture, with a potential entry into production within five years, subject to a positive feasibility study. This company is also active in Burkina Faso and Côte d'Ivoire.

These projects, which could more than double industrial gold production in the next five years, are the result of reforms in our country's investment framework and the demonstrated confidence of investors despite the ongoing Covid-19 pandemic.

The coming years will also be significant for iron ore, with projects like Simandou (which will likely see development with the *Transguinean Railway*) and Nimba (where implementation instruments with a new credible investor and operational evacuation agreement through Liberia are completed[27]), as well as for new substances

[27] The Implementation Agreement between the governments of Liberia and Guinea securing the use by Guinean mining operators of Liberian infrastructure and transport services was signed on October 11, 2019.

that have attracted noteworthy investments in research in recent years. This will mark a substantial step in diversifying mining production and enhancing the industry's resilience to fluctuations in commodity prices. Notably, this includes graphite, heavy metals, and base metals, and, of course, iron ore, provided market trends persist, and sector governance consolidates and continues to improve.

The maintenance of this momentum hinges on consolidating the reforms that have been implemented. These reforms clearly demonstrate the transformation that has taken place in the country's mines, driven by a clear political commitment at the highest level and consistent support from technical and financial partners such as the World Bank, IFC, UNDP, GIZ, etc. This support has materialized in:

- Adoption of a modern Mining Code that considers the responsible development issues of the mining sector, socio-economic and environmental impacts, and the balance of interests between investors and the state.
- Adoption of a Mining Policy Letter and the development of the Mining Sector Development Plan.
- Development of a master plan for shared infrastructure, aiming to reduce costs associated with mining projects.
- Establishment of a dedicated one-stop-shop for mining projects.
- Clean-up and modernization of the mining cadaster (now available online: www.guineecadastreminier.org).
- Alignment with the Extractive Industries Transparency Initiative (EITI)[28], including the publication of mining agreements on the internet. All mining contracts are published on the website www.contratsminiersguinee.org.

[28] https://eiti.org/countries/guinea

• Adoption of a Corporate Social Responsibility (CSR) policy and a policy to promote local content.

• Establishment of the Local Economic Development Fund (FODEL) and the National Fund for Local Development (FNDL) for the benefit of local communities.

The efforts made have led to the initiation of projects with a total value of $25 billion, drawing from exceptionally diverse sources of funding (United States, Germany, China, United Arab Emirates, Russia, United Kingdom, South Africa, Australia, India, etc.). In addition to mining companies, entities financing projects in Guinea include bi and multilateral financing institutions (International Finance Corporation (IFC), Multilateral Investment Guarantee Agency (World Bank Group), German Investment Corporation (UFK), Overseas Private Investment Corporation (OPIC-USA), African Development Bank, Export Development Canada) and some of the world's most demanding commercial institutions, such as Société Générale, BNP Paribas, Natixis, ING, etc.

That globally diverse picture of investors and lenders suggested a certain balance of interests in the Guinea's mines. It should first be noted that the government's mining policy has been in favor of the diversification of partnerships. In other words, any credible investor with a mutually beneficial viable project is welcome in Guinea, and in this case in the mining industry. Moreover, it is important to specify that the actual figures of ownership of resources and levels of investment contradict the allegations of quasi-monopoly of the Chinese entities. The bauxite resources of all the projects involving Chinese companies represented less than one third (1/3) of the bauxite resources allocated in the country's mines, while their investments exceeded two thirds (2/3) of all ongoing and planned investments in the sector. These resources held by Chinese entities (less than five billion tonnes) are smaller than those of the Compagnie des Bauxites de Guinée alone (nearly six billion tonnes) in which the State held 49 % of the shares. The fact is therefore that, with half of the shares of CBG, the Guinean State is one of the largest holders of bauxite reserves in the country! The other large known deposits (excluding CBG and Chinese companies together) with a billion tonnes or more are held by Australian, Russian and United Arab Emirates companies demonstrating, if need be, diversity in the control of Guinean bauxite resources.

In the iron ore industry, there is a certain balance of interests. The main deposits are those of Simandou (blocks 1 and 2, and blocks 3 and 4) and Nimba. Blocks 1 and 2 (potentially over one billion tonnes of iron ore) are controlled by Chinese interests; blocks 3 and 4 of Simandou (over 2 billion tonnes of iron ore) by the Anglo-Australian Rio Tinto as the main shareholder, despite a significant minority held by Chinese companies; and Nimba (potentially one billion tonnes, half of which is exploitable due to environmental constraints) by Western interests. Therefore, it can be said, without risk of error, that there is a certain balance of interests in the Guinean mining sector as a whole, even if the number of Chinese companies active in the bauxite industry may be misleading in this regard. Beyond the relative weight of companies from each origin in the sector, the most important aspect is the fair treatment of investors and the quality of relationships with companies, regardless of their country of origin. We have made the best efforts in this regard.

What should be highlighted for Guinea is the boom in the mines that has allowed an unprecedented level of job creation. The exponential growth in bauxite production (from less than 20 to over 80 million tonnes) has catapulted Guinea from 8% to 22% of global production, while the number of mining operations tripled. In parallel, the industry has created tens of thousands of jobs, more than doubled the state's direct mining revenues, and led to infrastructure development. Guinea has become the standard-bearer for the African mining vision, chosen to host the headquarters of the African Minerals Development Centre (AMDC) in 2018. The country revived the Guinea Mining Symposium (SMG), which has become the most popular mining event in Africa after the historic Indaba conference in South Africa. In 2019, the symposium welcomed over 600 delegates and more than 2,000 visitors from over forty countries. In 2019, the highly regarded Fraser Institute's report ranked the country's mining sector 20th in the world and first in Africa![29] This is a significant improvement from the 2015 edition[30], which ranked Guinea's mining sector only 103rd globally and 20th in Africa in terms of attractiveness for investments.

All the achievements in the sector at the end of this decade of reforms have, as their main foundation, the establishment and progressive consolidation of trust between investors/lenders and Guinea. This trust took time to build and still needs to solidify. However, it remains fragile—it is hard to gain but easy to lose. A country in an economic transition phase can go through virtuous or vicious circles until reaching a point of no return. It is not by chance that a relatively long time elapses between reforms and their positive effects on investment. When a state initiates reforms, the investor community begins by

---

[29] https://www.fraserinstitute.org/sites/default/files/annual-survey-of-mining-companies-2019.pdf

[30] https://www.fraserinstitute.org/sites/default/files/survey-of-mining-companies-2015.pdf

observing, gathering information, and assessing the scope and sustainability of the reforms. Then, the more daring investors start to invest, and others follow suit. The country gradually attracts more demanding investors and lenders, gaining a fragile good reputation. A virtuous circle opens. At the slightest major negative signal, investors wonder if the old demons are resurfacing. This signal could be armed conflict, a socio-political event, a challenge to state commitments, a deterioration in governance, etc. At the slightest adverse action, the more cautious or less advanced in their projects begin to stop investing or withdraw. Then others follow. And the country enters a vicious circle that leads to an eternal cycle of restarts. It is necessary to stay in the virtuous circle for a sufficient period to reach the point of no return in the development of the mines. Guinea has not yet reached this point. The transformation for added value, diversification for resilience, and infrastructure for optimizing investments are challenges in the development of the sector that make progress fragile.

13

Transparency as a tool for the irreversible development of the sector

Transparency in the mines is a key element in improving governance within the industry. Since 2011, with the adoption of the new Mining Code, transparency has been placed at the heart of the reform agenda. The publication of all mining contracts and Guinea's compliance with the Extractive Industries Transparency Initiative (EITI)[31] in 2014 marked a shift in an industry plagued by a level of opacity that did not reassure either the population or investors. Guinea, one of the first African countries to take this initiative, published mining contracts online, a measure that may seem insignificant today. However, this courageous decision was a response to popular demand, which was not necessarily well-received by various stakeholders. I was surprised by the tense reaction of our counterparts from a major international company when we informed them that the contract we were negotiating had to be published online. Despite applying appreciated governance standards, this company had concerns that were probably even stronger for less robustly governed companies, especially those not

[31] https://eiti.org/countries/guinea

publicly traded. I realized that the main concern was the disclosure of commercial and strategic information that competitors could use against the company. Despite these concerns, our counterparts, keen on preserving the company's good image, did not openly oppose this requirement, which was imposed on all miners in the country anyway. The systematic nature of publishing mining agreements reassured them about the fair nature of this measure, which also gave them access to the full content of their competitors' contracts. In any case, I understood the difficulty of changing habits in terms of transparency. If a company, having transparency as a governance principle for decades, has reservations about publishing its contracts, what about state agents who, for various reasons, have long felt comfortable with the opacity that prevailed in the sector? How did all the interest groups acting in the shadows—God knows there are some in the industry—react to this initiative? In any case, the process had become irreversible.

The irreversibility of transparency significantly contributes to the irreversibility of other reforms. This, from my perspective, is the ultimate utility of transparency and its main impact on the industry. Many see transparency simply as a constraint, the lifting of which allows for ticking boxes—a sacrifice made to appear good and gain points in governance evaluations. In reality, it is a powerful tool to make reforms irreversible. Once information is produced and actors get used to it, any regression triggers a spontaneous and strong reaction from these actors, forcing leaders to stay on course. When we started publishing the Mining Statistics Bulletin in December 2018, some mining companies were very reluctant to provide the requested statistical data, especially those related to their production. A few quarters later, the same companies were eager to provide the data and were now impatient to receive the bulletin to assess their performance compared to the competition.

Transparency is not merely a compliance measure with good governance criteria. It is a genuine instrument for building trust with all stakeholders and observers in the industry, a key tool to attract investments, and a powerful lever for the irreversibility of reforms. Transparency is gradually becoming ingrained in the habits of ministry officials, even in the day-to-day handling of cases by all relevant departments. The ministry has embraced this reform and implemented it with enthusiasm and conviction. However, this conviction and commitment did not make us lose sight of the risks associated with the form and scope of information to be made public. As an old Guinean leader used to say, "The state is not managed in public. It is managed responsibly." This responsibility requires that the timing and manner of sharing information be well-chosen to avoid the disclosure having an effect that undermines the ministry's goal, which is mining development. For example, when critical information about the content of negotiations with a mining company is disclosed before the end of the negotiation, it can weaken the state's negotiating position and prevent it from achieving the desired results. Adjustments in the negotiating strategy of the opposing company or interference from interest groups can, in this case, harm the interests of the state.

When agreements are negotiated, they are submitted to the entire government and the head of state through the Council of Ministers, and then to the National Assembly before being submitted to the Constitutional Court. This process allows elected representatives of the people, namely deputies and the President of the Republic, and all empowered institutions to express their views on the agreements in accordance with the laws in force. The obligation of transparency in disseminating the agreements arises after this process. Sharing the agreements with third parties before completing this process amounts to prejudging the opinion of the elected representatives of the people or the Constitutional Court on these agreements. Initiating a popular consultation on the agreements, especially with local communities, is simply a de facto denial of the mandate given to elected officials by the populations, including these same local communities. Nevertheless, some actors/observers recommend inserting a grassroots popular consultation into the contract adoption process, thereby de facto disregarding the mandates given by the populations themselves. It is necessary to consult communities at each phase of the project (particularly on social and environmental activities) as provided for in the regulations. However, the negotiations are intended to take place within a framework guaranteeing that the representatives of the population (the MPs and the Head of State) approve the results of the negotiations carried out by non-elected representatives of the State. In any case, the process adopted complies with the laws in force, some of which (notably the mining code) underwent broad consultations (including civil society) before their adoption.

Furthermore, the State also has the obligation to protect strategic and operational, commercial, and financial information of companies, without violating the laws in force. The disclosure of this information can sometimes harm, in an irreversible manner, the activities of these companies and the interests of the country.

It is therefore crucial for the Ministry of Mines to absolutely avoid a return to the culture of secrecy or provide any pretext to supporters of opacity, by relentlessly pursuing the transparency agenda. However, this should be done with respect for national institutions and considering the need to effectively fulfill the mission of developing the mines.

Transparency, beyond its positive effects on the governance aspects already discussed, is also an effective tool in the fight against corruption. Transparency facilitates the detection of wrongdoing due to its inappropriate or illegal nature. It simultaneously encourages actors to respect laws and procedures. It also alerts all stakeholders who fear or desire the analysis, interpretation, and use of the information published by industry actors and observers. Among these, NGOs and the press play a crucial role in using transparency to improve governance. However, it is essential to emphasize the need for these actors and observers to effectively collect and objectively process the publicly available information. The disappointing observation is that few actors, supposed to use public information, actually exploit it, even though they are aware of its availability. I have often been surprised by certain inaccurate analyses or comments on the industry while correct information is available in the public domain. Few, including those concerned with the subject matter, try to read, at least, the Mining Code and mining agreements available on the Internet, despite the ministry's efforts to provide the public with several key pieces of information.

Transparency, to fully serve the improvement of governance in the sector, must allow effective access to information for the main recipients (local populations, media, NGOs, etc.). Based on the inquiries made, it appears that only mining companies and international organizations diligently use the website where mining contracts are published. Mining companies often use it to request concessions from state negotiators in the name of fairness. A few rare national NGOs, when they have funded projects for this purpose, also seem to show interest. However, few media outlets and public officials appear to exercise their right to the available information. Nevertheless, no one can claim to have an acceptable knowledge of the industry, let alone be an expert, if they are not at least aware of the content of the Mining Code and the agreements that govern mining activities. More curiosity, rigor, and professionalism among national actors would enable transparency to play its role in the continuous and irreversible improvement of governance in the sector.

14

Necessary fight against corruption

During the meeting immediately following my assumption of office, I likely surprised my colleagues by directly addressing the issue of corruption in the mines. I tried to explain, in the simplest terms possible, the direct impact of corruption on the state but also on their respective lives. Indeed, when an official unduly grants a favor to a actor of the industry in exchange for the payment of a sum or an interest, it prevents the state from asserting all its rights due to the future loss incurred with that actor or the non-realization of a future investment compromised by the concession made to that investor. These conceded rights are a source of revenue for the state. This probable financial loss that the state incurs is likely to reduce its income, essential to meet the financing needs of hospitals, schools, roads, and salary increases that every civil servant, like each of my colleagues, as a Guinean, would have benefited from. So, it is the story of the snake biting its tail, as some would say. On that day, I even allowed myself a religious digression, referring to the divine punishment against high-ranking officials who often end their lives in total destitution after living in insolent opulence when they held high positions. The surprised looks of most of them gradually turned into questioning looks, then almost approving ones. Whether they were sincere or not, I intended to unfold an agenda of immediate and constant fight against corruption in the mines. My predecessor had done his best, but one minister is certainly not enough to defeat this scourge almost ingrained in daily customs at all levels of society.

The mining industry is a field of significant financial interests. Therefore, along with the oil and financial fields, it is more exposed to corruption than any other industry. Thus, combating this issue was considered a top priority. In addition to the losses in terms of essential revenue for financing the country's development, corruption undermines the credibility of the system and its actors, creating distortions harmful to investment. Equity and consistency in approach and actions are key elements in building trust among investors and encouraging them to make investment decisions. When an investor suspects that others may unduly receive favors that make them less competitive in the market, they may decide, in some cases, not to invest or, for many with fewer scruples, to use similar means to circumvent the rules. The result would be that only those investors willing to bypass the rules remain, and they would all eventually fail to abide by the rules. One consequence is that only a few projects of exceptional profitability would develop, with most mining title holders contenting themselves with speculation, leading to a quasi-stagnation of the sector. Another consequence is the entry of actors with low capacities and standards into the market. Therefore, the fight against corruption is not just a moral necessity. Like transparency, which also contributes to it, it is a means of ensuring the proper development of the mines.

Aware that my success as minister, which was an obligation, inevitably depended on this fight, I adopted a working method that ensured that the decisions made by the ministry were as objective as possible to eliminate the bias and subjectivity created by the corruption of one or more links in the chain. All files were reviewed at least two levels after processing (systematically) by the relevant technical department. Unless there was a general collusion, there was little chance that a single person, including myself, could push through a solution contrary to the interests of the country. This internal transparency has made the file processing more robust and ensured true information sharing and its appropriation by the stakeholders. Internal transparency is important to prevent any misinterpretation of actions and decisions by ministry officials, who are the first concerned with the implementation of projects, from creating any doubt about the files.

The other approach to combat corruption was to reduce, as much as possible, the excuses, whether admitted or not, that could be used to explain acts of corruption, failing an impossible justification. Ending the financing of the ministry missions by companies, especially control missions, and ensuring their full coverage by the ministry was one of these mechanisms. The other aspect of this approach concerned the fair provision of equipment and operating resources for all services, as far as possible. Finally, the collective needs of the staff, especially for transportation, were carefully addressed to ensure that the poorest (those without means of transportation) benefited from the availability of buses free of charge.

Corruption may occur when the opportunity is offered by the corrupter to a person who succumbs to the temptation thus created. Therefore, we put in place another mechanism that reduced the occurrence of "corruption opportunities" by limiting interference in private affairs. When a private actor sought a private partner to buy bauxite or gold, we simply provided them with a list and contacts of companies that matched their request, emphasizing that they had no obligation to report on the outcome of their negotiations, which were free if they complied with the law. The ministry's role was limited to approving the transaction if required by law, such as in the case of a transfer of shares. The same approach was observed in the case of conflicts between private actors. If no party had violated the regulations, the ministry's role was to facilitate discussion and ensure that the mining project was not affected, with private actors free to activate dispute resolution clauses in their agreements or take legal action in accordance with the law.

All these mechanisms can have their effect. However, the most deterrent mechanism in the fight against corruption is punishment. I made sure that the first proven cases of corruption were dealt with firmly to set an example. A department head who imprudently accepted payment from a company by check immediately faced the necessary sanctions, despite multiple interventions, with the decision disseminated within the ministry. As with cases of indiscipline or insubordination, handling the initial cases helped send a clear signal about my stance.

Acts of corruption are difficult to hide forever, especially in the mining industry where everyone talks about everyone to everyone. Setting an example and consistently giving a positive and clear signal helps, but the reputation that actors convey in various circles is the true barometer of the level of corruption. Testimonials from some investors about the decrease in the level of corruption in the mines in Guinea have greatly helped establish a reputation for the ministry and build confidence among investors. Permits would have been bought — even though the exploration permit is free in Guinea — by investors in the not-too-distant past. An investor who arrogated to himself the rights of a prince in violation of the rules long resisted joining the ranks because he thought, he later said, that certain dubious practices prevailing in the sector were still in place and therefore believed that we were making life difficult for him to obtain compensation. The bizarre conditions for obtaining his permit were enough to give chills. Like this investor, many sought to meet with the minister to be recommended for a permit with the technical services. After our insistence on the application of the "first come, first served" principle on free areas, they reluctantly followed the normal procedure (which was conspicuously displayed in our offices and on our sites) only to realize that they had wasted their time trying to meet the minister.

My predecessor, known for his rigor, seemed to have done his part of the work. I had to do my part and ensure that my successor would not have difficulty doing his as well. To succeed in completely eradicating the scourge, there must be a skillful combination of incentive and coercive measures. Incentive measures focus on improving the living and working conditions of civil servants. The ministry has done its best to improve working conditions, and even the lives of executives, as much as possible. Equipment, support for service operations, and the frequent missions of executives have contributed to this. Many executives have made efforts to follow the outlined path, demonstrating patriotic and responsible commitment. The state, as a whole, must assume its responsibility in creating minimal working and decent living conditions for its workers.

We have seen progress in the fight. However, the work must continue because, as long as the incentives and temptations remain intact, the evil will exploit the weaknesses of the "system" to thrive. This "system" is the real gangrene that makes any isolated action less or not effective and requires a comprehensive multisectoral approach.

"People can be bought." This is often heard from individuals who use it as an excuse to argue that corruption is like a fate to which everyone eventually succumbs. Even though perfection cannot be truly achieved, no excuse can validly justify corruption, especially on a large scale that is driven by a logic of enrichment at the expense of the state. Any system that does not combat corruption with the necessary means does not allow for prosperity. Corruption has a reward and a cost. The system must ensure that the cost of the corruption enterprise is always significantly higher than the reward that the protagonists (the corrupter and the corrupted) gain. The high probability, fairness, and rigor of the sanction are certainly the key to succeeding in this endeavor.

15.

Environmental and social impact: one of the biggest challenges

During a visit to the Simandou site in 2014, in Beyla[32], I was impressed by two things: the purity of the ore samples and the extraordinary greenery of the beautiful landscape of this mountain. Upon our return to Conakry, another member of the Simandou Working Group, of which I was a part, asked for my impressions after seeing the project sites on which we spent so much time working in the offices. He was obviously shocked that instead of discussing the exceptional iron ore content, I was complaining that we were obliged to destroy such a beautiful landscape for the needs of our development. I was not questioning the choice to develop this project, whose impacts, in terms of socio-economic development, would compensate for the environmental losses. My feelings, entirely legitimate, would have been more relevant if Guinea were at a much more advanced stage of its development, with immediate alternatives in terms of opportunities.

My instincts to preserve the environment also surfaced when, at the beginning of my term, I was presented with

---

[32] South East of Guinea

the country map showing active mining permits. "But where do the people live if there are permits covering all these parts of the territory?" I asked, noting the density of gold permits, to which the director had no clear answer.

Throughout my tenure as minister, I took an interest in environmental and social impact issues more out of instinct and personal inclination, with sincerity, than simply out of duty. Over the years, this issue has gained increasing importance in line with the accelerating pace of project development. We have thus become increasingly concerned with the ongoing conflict between the necessity of socio-economic development and the need for environmental preservation and offsetting social impacts.

The Mining Code and the Environmental Code impose on companies the obligation to carry out Environmental and Social Impact Assessments (ESIA) accompanied by an Environmental and Social Management Plan (ESMP). The purpose of this process is to identify, assess, and adopt actions to offset the negative impacts of mining activities on communities. It is based on the principle of grassroots consultations and review and validation by the competent authorities, namely the Guinean Office of Environmental Studies and Assessments (BGEEE) of the Ministry in charge of Environment. No mining exploitation permit is granted without the approval of the Ministry of the Environment based on work done and the documents submitted. Despite the existing shortcomings, the monitoring and control system is gradually improving through capacity building at the Guinean Office of Environmental Studies and Assessments (BGEEE).

Guinea has made significant progress in formalizing processes in recent years, including the adoption of a new Environmental Code in 2019 and specific guidelines on the implementation of this process. In parallel, the BGEEE has benefited from capacity building, notably with the support of the World Bank. However, it is important to acknowledge that the effective implementation of these regulations has always been insufficient, particularly regarding the monitoring of the effective implementation of ESMPs to offset impacts as the project is implemented.

To address this deficit, as part of environmental and social risk management, a strategic study on environmental and social impacts was conducted with the support of the World Bank, along with an independent assessment of the implementation of Environmental and Social Management Plans (ESMPs).

This evaluation of the implementation of ESMPs by mining companies in Guinea, conducted by an international firm, took place between October 2017 and May 2018. Although the initiative for such an assessment rested with the Ministry of Environment, it was initiated and funded by the Ministry of Mines, given our genuine concern for environmental and social risk management. However, we delegated the implementation of the assessment to the Ministry of Environment, which holds institutional responsibility for it. The evaluation covered the nine companies in the operational or advanced development phase at that time. The objectives of the study were to:

- Evaluate compliance with legal environmental assessment and management procedures (EIES, ESMPs).
- Assess the level of effective implementation of ESMPs.
- Estimate residual impacts on biophysical and human environments.
- Assess the level of monitoring and evaluation developed by government services.
- Propose improvement measures.

Thanks to this initiative, we were able to obtain an objective monitoring base for impact management, which was made available to the Ministry of the Environment. On our part, we ensured that all companies were questioned about their shortcomings and, within the limits of our capacities, monitored the implementation of the recommendations. In parallel, several missions were organized with the Ministry of the Environment to address nuisances and other environmentally harmful actions reported by various sources.

This collaboration with the Environmental Services has led to increased attention to environmental issues and has improved over the years the management of impacts, especially concerning dust control in the Boké region. Infrastructure development and the adoption of new emission management approaches have been implemented. This includes the construction of 17 km of paved roads, strengthening the fleet of tanker trucks for watering, and the use of new procedures (speed limitations) and special products on certain mining roads to limit dust emissions. The government has also initiated the construction of the Boké bypass road project to reduce nuisances experienced by the population. Some companies have even completely revised their Environmental and Social Management Plan in response to the actions we have taken. In any case, the construction of railway infrastructure, especially the 125 km railway under construction between Santou (Boffa) and Dapilon (Boké)[33], should significantly reduce the risk of dust emissions from mining trucks in the region on mining roads. This transformation, beneficial economically and for reducing nuisances, however, requires effective consideration of the impact of changes in the transport model on economic opportunities in transportation, especially the nature of jobs.

[33] The North West region of Guinea.

Another issue that has caught our attention is the compensation of impacted populations. The lack of regulatory framework in this area is one of the shortcomings that we have worked to address. To this end, a framework for the compensation and resettlement of populations affected by mining projects is in the final stages of completion. This document took more than a year to finalize due to the government's relevant choice to adopt a fully inclusive process in its development. The implementation will manage, within a sustainable approach, the compensation of affected populations. The exclusive reliance on financial compensation, in some cases, has shown its limitations. Financial compensations tend to create socio-economic distortions in communities, and ultimately, the beneficiaries may fall into precarious situations by abandoning their traditional livelihood activities, coupled with the use of funds in activities that do not durably replace these traditional activities.

The management of environmental and social impacts, along with economic impacts, represents the greatest challenge for Guinea's mines in the years to come. The mining policy aims not only for the responsible exploitation of natural resources but, more importantly, the gradual independence of the country's economy from the mines. Mines provide the best immediate opportunity for the development of Guinea, serving as its most effective lever for integrated development. To succeed in this endeavor, continued efforts in impact management are necessary.

It is true that the physical impact of mines is one of the most spectacular, even though mining itself covers less than 6% of the national territory. Despite this relatively limited proportion of land occupation, there has been a continuous expansion of the total area covered by bauxite permits due to incessant requests on pristine lands over the years. To curb this harmful trend to the environmental protection agenda, especially when we had already granted enough bauxite permits to achieve production and processing objectives, I issued a decree suspending the granting of bauxite exploration permits on pristine lands.

Beyond the need to preserve the country's natural capital, the objective is also to give the best chance of success to the current mining policy by ensuring peaceful and fruitful coexistence between mining companies and the communities hosting their operations. The effective implementation of the Natural Resources, Mining and Environmental Management Project (PGRNME)[34], a $65 million project with the support of the World Bank, for capacity building and impact management, will significantly contribute to this dynamic.

---

[34] https://projects.worldbank.org/en/projects-operations/project-detail/P168613

16

Artisanal Gold Mining: a risky opportunity

While industrial mining operations pose risks to the environment and society, artisanal gold mining is creating increasing social tensions and environmental pressure. The sight of almost lunar landscapes in certain areas and the evident pollution of certain watercourses have shocked everyone. Upon taking office in January 2016, I dispatched a secret mission to the artisanal gold mining areas to understand the realities of this activity. Beyond the well-known environmental and social damage, the most surprising conclusion of this mission was the level of organization and complicity among all local actors in this parallel economy that involves several hundred thousand people. The social and economic weight of the activity required a reform to make this exploitation more environmentally and socially responsible. We immediately initiated consultations with the National Union of Artisanal Gold Miners of Guinea (UNOG) to start the reform.

In this context, the National Artisanal Miners' Day was organized in Kankan (North-East of Guinea) on February 6, 2017. Several missions of consultations and awareness-raising took place in the prefectures of the region in the months leading up to this national day. The objectives of these missions were to diagnose the sector, explain the spirit of the reform aimed at improving current practices, apply the participatory approach that should prevail in the reform to consider the concerns and experience of the sector's key players. These consultations, along with the support of the Artisanal Gold Council and other experts mobilized with the assistance of the World Bank, allowed us to define a roadmap for the reform.

This adopted roadmap relied on essential actions for the reorganization of artisanal gold mining activity:

- The search for corridors reserved for artisanal exploitation in consultation with artisanal miners and their provision to them. One of the fundamental difficulties for artisanal gold mining is the insufficient reserved areas, making the age-old practice unregulated, or even illegal. Consequently, areas have gradually been reserved in prefectures with high artisanal activity.
- The establishment of rules for artisanal mining, considering the types of equipment that can be used, site rehabilitation, the prohibition of child labor, secure mining methods, the non-use of chemicals, etc.
- The establishment, in each prefecture, of a technically-oriented team dedicated to artisanal mining, trained, equipped, and dedicated to the administration, monitoring, and control of sector activities to ensure compliance with regulations governing artisanal mining.
- The census of individuals involved in artisanal mining for better identification and supervision of these actors by professional category.
- Sensitization and formalization of actors into economic interest groups.
- Facilitation, support, and business matchmaking with partners willing to provide financial and technical means in accordance with defined and accepted protocols

and governance supervised by the Ministry of Mines and Geology.

Despite this seemingly robust framework, we quickly realized the magnitude of the challenges in the practical feasibility of the proposed solutions. Finding a model that has already proven successful on a large scale was the main challenge for all countries where artisanal mining existed, and Guinea was no exception. We decided to initiate several pilot projects, the experiences of which would be capitalized on to develop a model that provides guarantees, especially in terms of profitability for artisanal miners, the safety of stakeholders, and environmental protection.

One project was set up with a private partner who chose a production-sharing scheme that seemed to satisfy all parties. Unfortunately, this scheme suffered from technical difficulties and the abusive financial demands of some actors. Another project was implemented in parallel with German cooperation (GIZ), which provided equipment and technical assistance. Besides profitability issues, this scheme particularly suffered from disagreements among group members and their failure to uphold their commitments. A third model was initiated with a mining company planning to relocate artisanal activities from its active mining zones. Three years later, this initiative had not yet yielded the expected results.

In any case, the progress made by the various experimented models has not, after several years, led to a model that meets the expectations of all parties involved. Several factors explain this situation, starting with internal technical difficulties within the ministry that have hindered progress toward a model that provides all the necessary guarantees. One of our mistakes was underestimating the technical and financial resources needed to ensure the richness of the mining area for profitability. A pilot program for internal geological research was initiated to address this deficiency, although scaling up would require financial resources that the ministry does not currently have.

Additionally, three years of internal leadership battles within the National Union of Artisanal Gold Miners of Guinea (UNOG) also delayed the progress of the artisanal mining reform agenda. This open battle, initiated in 2018, only concluded in August 2020 with the election of a new national bureau for the UNOG. During this period, the transitional team's sole mandate was to organize elections. Therefore, we did not have legitimate counterparts to advance the reform.

Another challenge in the artisanal mining reform is the lack of understanding among the most active parties regarding the essence of the reform. The actors, advocating for the interests of artisanal miners, are not themselves genuine miners for the most part. The commercial chain of artisanal mining begins with *artisanal miners* in the mines, who sell to *scale operators* (those equipped with small scale scales for weighing). These scale operators sell to *collectors* who, in turn, sell to *export counter* owners. The counter owners are the only ones authorized to export gold to their foreign clients. It turns out that most of the actors dominating the organizations are collectors or counter owners, thus participants at the end of the marketing chain. These active participants do not necessarily advocate for the interests of all chain actors, especially those upstream (those working in the mine). It is as if workers were defended by their employers since collectors and counter owners contribute to the pre-financing and organization of the activity at the grassroots level. The conflict of interest means that the profits of actors downstream are often more defended than those of actors upstream who are the real targets of the reform. This situation creates tensions in negotiations with UNOG representatives and a certain disconnect between the concerns of the state's interlocutors and the realities on the ground.

Furthermore, those among the "artisanal miners" who want to engage in mining, in truth, mostly do not wish to do so according to the modalities specified by the current regulations. They do not want to mine either in the true artisanal sense or following the semi-industrial scheme intended for small mechanized operations. They want to enjoy the benefits of artisanal mining applied to a mechanized operation, exempting them from the required technical, commercial, environmental, and social requirements.

The last, and not the least, pitfall involves local complicity in the opening of so-called artisanal mines which, in practice, are often wild mechanized operations or makeshift wild mines. Efforts are often hindered by complicity at various levels that benefit from the revenue of these operations, which have a direct harmful impact on health, the environment, and, even worse, on miners who often lose their lives in galleries built and operated in violation of any basic safety rules. Traditional, age-old methods of artisanal mining have given way to mass exploitation involving the use of chemicals with new dangerous techniques imported from abroad. In addition, the illicit use of medical and narcotic products has become a scourge in communities hosting artisanal mines.

This seemingly bleak picture, however, is not a foregone conclusion. The establishment of the new national executive office of the UNOG, which appears very willing to progress on the census of gold miners, could bring about this initiative, which can only be effectively carried out within the framework of an organized chain from the bottom to the top. To achieve this, it will certainly be necessary for the members of the new office to consider the interests of actors throughout the chain, especially those of the gold miners at the base. Also, lessons learned from pilot projects will hopefully lead to progress in the reform of artisanal gold mining in the coming years through the identification of a profitable and responsible model that can be generalized nationwide. The effective reservation of gold mining areas and the parceling in certain localities are achievements, as is the establishment of effectively functional supervisory teams in localities.

However, there will likely be a need for exceptional financial resources to support the reforms, especially in geological research and assistance in acquiring basic equipment. These resources could be generated by reinstating the export tax on artisanal gold, the revenues of which can be directly allocated to a fund for promoting responsible artisanal mining. This scheme, whose details and implementation mechanism must be thoroughly examined beforehand, could have the advantage of facilitating the mobilization of new resources directly related to artisanal mining. The fund would finance not only the modernization of the artisanal sector but also the transformation of associations into semi-industrial operations as provided for in the mining code.

At the same time, awareness-raising efforts should be continued, accompanied by support for stakeholders to choose authorized operations, especially semi-industrial mining that can be the subject of partnerships with local expert offices for assistance in studies. Additionally, the reform could involve examining the feasibility (technical, environmental, and safety) and relevance of introducing a small-scale mining model (mechanized) between traditional artisanal mining and semi-industrial mining, while avoiding simply legalizing current illegal mechanized operations that do not meet minimum standards in terms of safety and environmental and social impact management.

Lastly, to curb complicity in illegal operations, in addition to administrative and judicial sanctions, a portion of the Local Economic Development Fund (FODEL) resources could be invested in supporting the retraining of actors in other income-generating activities, particularly in agriculture. FODEL could also support local environmental protection actions and provide technical assistance to artisanal miners through allocation decisions made by local authorities.

In addition to industrial mining, artisanal mining, along with agriculture, constitutes the primary economic activity for a significant portion of the active population in several prefectures. The population of artisanal miners in Guinea is estimated to be over 200,000 people. Besides creating employment, artisanal mining serves as a source of foreign currency for Guinea, contributing to the stability of the national currency, not to mention the induced economic effects. Beyond its impacts, both positive and negative, on community life, artisanal mining, like other activities involving interactions with mining companies, is a source of tensions and conflicts with these companies, mainly due to the intrusion of artisanal miners in mining concessions. Ensuring harmonious coexistence between artisanal miners and mining companies, and more broadly between communities and companies, remains a major challenge in the sector that deserves special attention.

17

Relations between mining companies and communities

The quality of relationships between mining companies and the communities in which they operate is a crucial element for the sustainable success of mining development. Challenges in this regard involve not only compliance with the obligations of the companies and their actions within the framework of Corporate Social Responsibility (CSR), but also, and more importantly, the effective management of the expectations of the local populations.

Guinea is one of the few African countries to have formalized its Corporate Social Responsibility (CSR) policy in mining in 2017. This policy incorporates best practices in all aspects of CSR. CSR refers to the mandatory and voluntary actions that companies undertake, in the spirit of being a 'citizen' enterprise, for effective and responsible management of environmental, social, and economic activities and impacts, promoting sustainable exploitation. It also enables the company to obtain what is commonly referred to in industry jargon as the 'social license' to operate.

In many cases, companies themselves have an internal Corporate Social Responsibility (CSR) policy, particularly within multinational corporations, which benefit from a robust governance system for this purpose. Within this framework, they have an annual budget for community intervention to finance projects typically agreed upon with community representatives. These projects may involve social activities such as the construction of health centers, schools, wells, etc., the implementation of health campaigns, or economic empowerment activities for youth and women. In the event of disasters, companies may also carry out unplanned emergency interventions. All these interventions are voluntary and do not fall under the legal obligations of these companies.

Despite the efforts made by all stakeholders involved, it is common for tensions to arise between companies and local communities. Some of these tensions occasionally escalate into tragedies, resulting in material losses and, in rare cases, loss of human lives.

My time at the head of the Ministry of Mines has allowed me to observe how fragile the relationships between a mining company and the neighboring local community can be. Peace can be incredibly precarious. This fragility can be further heightened by a mining boom for which none of the actors are adequately prepared. Whether it is the government, whose capacities are strained and take time to adjust to an increased demand for mediation, or the companies that, absorbed by time and budget constraints, do not pay enough attention to the smoldering discontent around them. It is also true for the communities themselves, who, placing all their hopes on the sweep and hum of machinery in their usually quiet locality, are torn between this hope and the disappointment that all their problems related to employment, income, and socio-economic infrastructure do not disappear overnight.

This precarious, and even detrimental, situation turns into a crisis marked by threats, blockades, and regrettable attacks in many cases. Over the years, although the frequency of crises has decreased, for a long time, we faced an average of at least one crisis per week, often leading to activity shutdowns. The extent, frequency, and intensity of these crises were such that, beyond administrative pressure, there was genuine psychological pressure. A company director in conflict with the host community, which had blocked all activities, came to appreciate the efforts necessary to contain such a crisis. 'I now realize what you go through on a sector-wide scale,' he told me, almost with compassion. He was even more surprised when I revealed the frequency of such crises.

The tension and efforts invested in relations with communities were comparable to those of all other issues in the sector. With the Minister of Territorial Administration, governors, prefects, and sub-prefects, we were often faced with what I would describe as a frontline. Like in a powder keg, all it took was a spark for a crisis to erupt. The spark could be the dismissal of an employee, a false rumor, the agitation of a handful of job seekers, a delay in a community project, the manipulation of a businessman seeking a contract, and so on. Any incident that, under normal circumstances, can be controlled by the intervention of a company representative. However, conditions are often far from normal. The lack of basic socio-economic infrastructure and endemic unemployment exacerbated by a massive influx of Guineans from all parts seeking employment create latent tension that is not solely related to mining activities. The conditions for repetitive crises are often present long before the company is established. The presence of a mining company multiplies expectations. The clumsiness of sometimes approximate management of community relations by the company exacerbates a form of frustration or bitterness within the community.

Even if the mining company acts through its community development budget to meet certain basic socio-economic infrastructure needs, that task obviously falls primarily to the State. The company undertakes voluntary actions to guarantee good neighborliness. It has the obligation to pay the taxes to the State. But it does not have the vocation, the obligation, to build roads, schools, health centers, wells, outside the requirements of the Environmental and Social Management Plan intended to compensate for the impacts of its activities. Nor does the company have the obligation—nor the ability—to recruit the entire labor force from within the community. She recruits according to her needs. The creation of jobs at the community, city, and national level, to reduce unemployment, is the responsibility of the State, through the development of public and commercial activities and projects. Not to mention that unemployment within the community is exacerbated by the return of many young people to the village from Conakry (and elsewhere). The sudden population growth of communities hosting new mining operations is a phenomenon that even the state could not prevent due to the freedom of movement of citizens. However, it is a phenomenon that significantly marks the community on the social, economic, and cultural levels. A village of just 1,000 people that hosted a mining company in 2015 ended up with more than 10,000 people in less than two years, creating extraordinary pressure on the community's socio-economic infrastructure, to the point that water wells built by the mining company could no longer meet the community needs.

The story of Kamsar (Boké region) is the typical example of these migratory flows creating an exponential demand for basic social services. That village of less than 10,000 inhabitants in the sixties has become a city of at least 300,000 inhabitants in less than half a century. The sub-prefecture of Kintinian, in Siguiri, with approximately 150,000 inhabitants, is more populated than several other prefectures in Guinea. The phenomenon is common to all mining localities. The only solution is to increase investment in socio-economic infrastructure to accommodate that population growth, beyond the direct impact of mining activities. This is where the judicious use of the Local Economic Development Fund (FODEL), supplied by the local contribution of companies for the benefit of impacted communities, and the National Local Development Fund (FNDL), the amount of which is based on the population of each community, is crucial to effectively compensate for the indirect impacts of mining activity arising from migration to these communities. This is in addition to improving the living conditions of the populations already present when mining companies are established. Social infrastructure (water wells, schools, health centers), economic infrastructure (bridges, roads, markets, etc.), and income-generating activities (agricultural and livestock projects, cold rooms for product preservation, small processing units, etc.) are thus implemented for this purpose. The sustainability of these funds, replenished annually, will gradually address shortcomings on all fronts, except for major investments in basic socio-economic infrastructure covered by the national budget. Heavy investments such as large bridges and road paving cannot be carried out with these funds. These major infrastructures, beyond the capacity of both the FODEL and the FNDL of a community to undertake, are therefore implemented under the national development budget, under the responsibility of the State.

It is true that the demands of communities are often legitimate, and the impatience is understandable, but these requests are sometimes directed at the wrong interlocutor (the mining company instead of the State) regarding basic social services. The methods are sometimes inappropriate, and communities are often manipulated by influence peddlers within them or among nationals living in the capital, Conakry, or abroad. Some of these individuals have occasionally created non-governmental organizations (NGOs) intended to negotiate on behalf of the community with the company and authorities, in place of local elected officials, traditional, religious, and administrative authorities. These NGOs are often commercial enterprises or represent such entities seeking contracts from the company, abusing the trust of the community as a prodigal child promising them all the prosperity in the world if a contract is obtained. How do you explain to families that their son or daughter is only seeking their own interests and not that of the community when there are dozens of unemployed youths among them? We have often succeeded in this only through awareness campaigns, but also by being firm on the necessity of legitimacy of the interlocutors when awareness becomes ineffective.

When a mine is opened in a locality, it creates the illusion of an El Dorado where all employment and development issues will be solved. The disproportionate, even utopian, expectations in some cases must be carefully managed by both the government and the mining company. Consultations conducted by the company in collaboration with government services should help limit these expectations to a reasonable level. Often, the stakeholders, especially the company's personnel, underestimate the importance of prior awareness in managing expectations.

I remember the managing director of a small semi-industrial gold mining operation promising to hire all the youth from a locality with over 100,000 inhabitants (with at least tens of thousands of young people seeking employment). During a visit to the site, I was surprised by the number of curious young people accompanying us. I took the opportunity to ask the company's representative to tell the truth to the young people, whom I took as witnesses. The truth was that this company would barely employ a few hundred people and certainly would not address all the community's problems, as its officials suggested. It is not uncommon to see officials or company representatives being imprudent or irresponsible, not being clear enough about the limits of what mining activity can bring to the community. Promising little and delivering much, instead of promising much and delivering little, should be the rule in every circumstance. Some opt for the easier path initially, which eventually catches up with the company, creating a conflict-ridden atmosphere around it.

The management of expectations must be continuous, with a competent and responsible community relations department within the company, supported consistently by local authorities. This department should be proactive and transparent, taking responsibility for anticipating issues. The collection of information on complaints and their diligent management (responding with actions or precise explanations) is necessary. The effectiveness of this management is also contingent on the understanding of local culture and traditions by community management agents and officials.

Beyond the legal obligations related to local content, it is essential that those responsible for community relations have a thorough knowledge of the culture and traditions of the covered communities. The primary responsible person and agents in direct contact with the community should speak the local dialect and, as much as possible, have lived in these localities or similar ones. This is necessary to establish a relationship of trust and overcome language barriers with predominantly illiterate populations.

The relaunch, in July 2017, by the government, through the refreshment of the mechanism, of Committees for Consultation in Mining Localities (CCLM), responds to the imperative of establishing a relationship of trust in addition to the internal mechanism of mining companies. These committees, composed of representatives of each stakeholder in the community, are tasked with preventing and intervening in conflict resolution through dialogue. We have been able to establish CCLMs in about a hundred municipalities in all regions, with the support of the United Nations Development Programme (UNDP), German cooperation (GIZ), and Search for Common Ground.

The establishment of CCLMs in the remaining municipalities and the effective and permanent operationalization of this consultation framework, which has suffered from insufficient means for implementation, and the effective institutional support of CCLMs by local authorities and elected officials, will contribute to strengthening peace in mining localities through a mastery of the expectations of each party and mutual understanding.

The origin of most conflicts in the sector is the considerable gap between expectations and real possibilities, mainly due to poor communication quality between companies and communities. The major crisis in Boké (northwest of the country) in April 2017 is an example of the gap between the expectations of the population on one hand, and the obligations and intervention capacities of the companies on the other hand. It was precisely related to the issue of basic socioeconomic infrastructure. Violent uprisings began in the urban municipality on Monday, April 24, 2017, involving attacks against public buildings, roadblocks, disruptions to the mineral railway, and clashes with law enforcement services.

The uprisings were triggered by a breakdown in the power plant supplying the city, primarily due to an overload on the capacity of the facilities. This overload was mainly a result of a doubling of electricity demand between 2016 and 2017, which the existing facilities could not adequately meet.

Realizing the severity of the situation and the failure of all initiatives taken during the first three days of the uprising, I had to urgently travel to Boké on April 27. It was a perilous journey, following violent attacks on local personalities just days earlier. We decided to travel at night with scouts confirming the absence of ambushes along the way. Among the demonstrators, there were troublemakers who were responsible for most of the violence. It was crucial to avoid any situation that could lead to mistakes by the security services accompanying the delegation. We arrived at Kamsar, the chosen base, in the middle of the night without any incidents.

The information received from various sources indicated that beyond the issue of electricity supply (which was the urgent demand) and water, there was a general unease related to youth employment (especially by mining companies), the disturbances caused by trucks passing through the city (hence the demand for the construction of a bypass road), and the judicious use of funds allocated by mining companies for local development contributions.

Following various consultations between the delegation, the ministry staff (who were dispatched to the field as soon as the information was received), local authorities, and people of the locality residing in Conakry, it was decided to organize a meeting with all stakeholders. On Saturday, April 29, 2017, the community center (in the center of Boké) served as the venue for this meeting with all the relevant actors.

The atmosphere was tense upon our arrival, with local authorities and high-ranking officials from the national gendarmerie in attendance. The adults had positioned themselves in the front rows, and the young "protesters" were at the back of the room. The latter were easily recognizable by their dazed looks, darkened by several sleepless nights, and their clothes completely soiled from their activities in the streets. The spokesperson for the protesters took the floor in a vindictive tone to list the demands, which had grown from half a dozen to about thirty points, with redundancies suggesting that several opportunistic groups had infiltrated the original group at the last moment.

After the spokesperson for the participants presented the list of demands, I took the floor to first strongly condemn the acts of violence and to alert on the consequences it could have on the government's ability to improve living conditions for the people of Guinea in general and Boké in particular.

I then provided detailed explanations for each of the points, outlining the ongoing and planned actions by the government, highlighting the illegal/unreasonable nature of some demands, and promising to report back to the government. In a frank and direct language that displeased many participants, I endeavored to demonstrate authority, leaving no room for any perception of weakness from the authorities we represented. This language was reinforced by a deliberate posture. I stood up and spoke while walking between the aisles of the room, physically confronting the protesters who, in my opinion, needed to understand that the State was not afraid. A genuine psychological confrontation, especially with the young people at the back of the room, ensued to assert dominance over the audience. I particularly emphasized, in a room that we were gradually gaining control over, the necessity of ending all forms of violence and removing roadblocks before engaging in any discussion on the points of contention.

In turn, representatives of the various groups demanded, at the very least, the resolution of the electricity-related demand before any suspension of the movement. To my surprise, some individuals whom we had entrusted with the mediation mission just days earlier revealed their duplicity to the point of threatening to detain the delegation if electricity was not provided every night. With straightforward language, we made it clear to them that no threat would compel us to make a promise that was impossible to fulfill. Faced with the impossibility of meeting their main demand, the protesters decided to peacefully halt all mining activities in the prefecture until their point was effectively addressed. Barely had the meeting ended when numerous roadblocks began to be erected throughout the city.

Informal discussions and awareness-raising missions involving multiple stakeholders were initiated to defuse the situation and facilitate a calm dialogue. Initially, it was decided to avoid direct contact with the protesters. Therefore, intermediary figures were used to communicate with the dissenting groups. Subsequently, we received troubling information about the activities of some of our mediators and other individuals working to undermine our efforts. We were ultimately forced to acknowledge the failure of this approach.

On May 1, 2017, we opted for a different approach without intermediary figures, using field agents to engage with the actors involved in the protests while continuing awareness campaigns through the media. The attrition efforts eventually paid off: on Monday, May 1, 2017, the roadblocks were lifted, and direct discussions took place with key stakeholders and our teams.

As agreed by the parties, on May 2, 2017, a monitoring committee was established under the leadership of local authorities. This committee worked on May 3, 2017, with officials from the Ministry of Mines and Geology to review the various points of contention. The points related to the Ministry of Mines and Geology were the subject of an action plan (indicating ongoing actions, upcoming actions, and anticipated completion deadlines) endorsed by all parties during this session. These were, in fact, prioritized actions already included in the Ministry of Mines' work plan, not new actions initiated due to negotiations. Participants simply insisted that all points of contention be submitted to the government for review. We were able to defuse the crisis without definitively resolving it. Measures taken later by the Ministry of Energy and regular communication with the movement's leaders, within the framework of a monitoring committee, helped restore trust and calm before the next crisis, as is often the case with demands related to basic socioeconomic infrastructure that can only be satisfied over several years. Members of this monitoring committee, leaders of the protesters, faced criticism from those who chose them, accusing them of being turned against the movement. In fact, these representatives of the protesters, in good faith, had simply understood, through our regular exchanges, that the government was already making reasonable efforts on most of the demands. They thus became objective intermediaries with the various groups.

The lack of information often leads to many misunderstandings and crises. The state, through its central and decentralized structures, must constantly have an effective information network and a system of regular communication. This system is even more important as we observe, over the years and with the exponential growth of mining activities, the emergence of new "experts" in the mining industry. These include some nationals who have a status as influencers, advisers to community opinion leaders. Most of them are extremely useful in establishing a climate of peaceful coexistence. Better informed, they participate in raising awareness among communities about their rights and the legal approach to grievances, while alerting authorities at all levels. However, a few of them misuse this privileged position to disseminate false information, sometimes pursuing personal interests, making communities believe that demanding through violent protests is the only solution to obtain what is rightfully theirs from the companies. There are also some members of the press who, without seeking contradictory information, disseminate incorrect information about mining activities. To enhance the objectivity of media coverage in the industry, we organized a training for journalists on mining governance in Kindia from January 25 to 27, 2019. The participation of 50 journalists representing most media outlets in this workshop provided a sufficient level of information to journalists on the challenges, constraints, results, and prospects of mining development in Guinea. This workshop significantly improved the relevance and objectivity of media coverage of mining issues in almost all outlets. Contrary to our assumptions, bad faith was not the main cause of biased media coverage in the industry. It was rather a lack of information.

Finally, these new "experts" also include some NGOs that, in their quest for material to fund their programs or justify their funding, carry out biased and unverified interventions, often criticizing activities in the sector under the guise of whistleblowers. I am convinced that civil society must complement and even monitor the actions of all stakeholders in the industry, including the government. However, the seal of independence cannot be a pretext for shirking the societal responsibility they bear in Guinea's socioeconomic development process. Some seem to underestimate the impact of a negative article or a biased "study" on investment in the sector. Investors, in their search to make investment decisions, can easily be deterred by access to negative information. No one will complain if the information is true, but it must indeed be accurate.

However, it must be acknowledged that the work of many organizations (press and NGOs) aiming to genuinely contribute to healthy debate and transparency is ultimately not fully appreciated due to a few bad actors. It is therefore crucial that the efforts of these serious and professional organizations be supported and promoted through sincere collaboration so that good examples can help improve the overall environment. At our level, we have consistently sought to involve the press in our activities and NGOs in our consultations, as is indeed mandated in certain cases by the Mining Code.

The regular confusion created by certain actors presenting themselves as neutral, while acting for political or financial interests, hampers the development of the mines, which relies on private investments. The paradox is that those who disseminate incorrect and biased information about the industry are often the first to complain about its lag. This is, however, the creation of a circle, either virtuous or vicious. It is important to move forward openly and not claim neutrality, allowing the audience to judge information with the right perspective. It is simply a matter of demonstrating responsibility, as one is entitled to expect from all sector stakeholders. Accountability is not only applicable to the state; it concerns all actors in the public sphere.

18

Local content: confusion and misunderstanding

The origin and reason for the persistence of tensions and crises between host communities and mining companies are often economic. Unemployment, the lack of entrepreneurial activities, and market opportunities play a significant role. In addition to impact compensation activities carried out by companies, FODEL and FNDL projects, the promotion of "local content" is an effective tool for reducing tensions by employing Guineans from the host community and other areas and creating market opportunities for their businesses.

The promotion of local content is at the core of the policy pursued by the state since 2011, especially with its effective consideration in the Mining Code. It represents a key channel for the actual realization of the expected benefits of the mining industry on the national economy, particularly in improving the living conditions of Guineans. In this regard, it is important to have a precise understanding of the concept of local content, which is subject to two significant confusions.

The first notable confusion lies in the distinction between local content and local or community development. Unlike the concept of local or community development, which focuses on the implementation of collective socioeconomic development projects within communities, local content relates to the employment of Guineans in companies and the local purchases made by mining companies from Guinean SMEs.

As part of corporate social responsibility, mining companies allocate an annual budget for the implementation of local development projects funded on a voluntary basis by these companies. These projects may include water wells, rural roads, health centers, schools, markets, or income-generating activities (especially in horticulture or livestock). The implementation of these projects generally focuses on compensating for impacts within the framework of Environmental and Social Management Plans (ESMP) or voluntarily, as part of promoting good neighborly relations with communities and humanitarian efforts.

Thus, the implementation of collective projects (commercial or non-commercial) in communities falls within the realm of local development. As for local content, it focuses on the employment and promotion of Guinean nationals within the company, as well as local purchases. Article 108 of the Mining Code sets specific quotas for these purposes for job categories and the phase of activity (exploration, development, and operation) of the company. Additionally, local content also involves the procurement of goods and services from Guinean companies. Article 107 of the Mining Code, dealing with preference for Guinean companies, also sets the proportion of local purchases for the three phases of activity (exploration, development, and operation) of the company. The notion of Guinean companies is clearly defined as those owned or controlled by Guineans, meaning those in which Guinean nationals hold more than 50% of the capital. The reminder of this shareholder qualification is not always superfluous. It is not uncommon for some to consider, under the local content requirements, companies registered in Guinea whose capital may be more than 50% owned by foreigners.

The second common confusion in promoting local content relates to the interpretation of the term "local." Many, especially among residents and natives of the areas surrounding mining operations, believe that local content exclusively pertains to the localities hosting mining companies. On this basis, they argue that jobs and procurement contracts should only be granted to the sons and daughters of the region. However, from a strictly legal standpoint, local content primarily concerns individuals of Guinean nationality, regardless of their specific location within Guinea. Moreover, Guineans are free to establish residence and work anywhere in Guinea.

While it is legitimate for the sons and daughters of a region to expect preference in local jobs and procurement contracts, and financially beneficial for companies to act in this way to reduce certain costs, the promotion of what can be termed "*local local content*" (in contrast to "*national local content*") must be done judiciously to avoid intercommunity tensions. Some argue that, all else being equal, priority should be given to the community hosting the mine, as it directly experiences its impacts. However, it is essential to bear in mind that existing regulations and practices already provide mechanisms for compensating impacts, namely mandatory and voluntary local development actions, as well as the Local Economic Development Fund, which is funded by a direct levy on the turnover of companies solely for the benefit of impacted local communities.

For centuries, internal migrations have been observed in Guinea as people search for economic opportunities in the mining industry, especially in artisanal gold mining.

For several decades, similar migrations have been noted towards industrial and semi-industrial mining areas. Initially, this was for bauxite mining in Kassa island from 1937, iron mining in Kaloum (in the capital city) from 1939, and later in other localities where profound demographic changes accompanied these migrations, sometimes transforming villages into towns. Guineans have welcomed other Guineans to their ancestral lands in the context of mining operations, sharing in the benefits of mining. Today, other Guineans are hosting fellow Guineans whose ancestors may have been welcomed by others in the past. Tomorrow, these initial hosts could be welcomed by other Guineans. These migrations are inherent to the finite nature of mining resources and mining cycles. For mining exploitation to contribute to the consolidation of Guinea's social unity instead of fueling division, it should be natural for Guineans, beyond strict legal enforcement, to be considered and accepted throughout Guinea in their pursuit of economic opportunities (employment and contracts) in the mines. Otherwise, there is a risk of witnessing situations that, beyond their gravity, challenge the rule of hospitality, which is a heritage to preserve. We emphasized this reminder of hospitality during a reconciliation mission between two villages in dispute over the employment of their respective residents by a mining company. At the establishment of the first company, residents of the first village vigorously requested that recruitment be limited exclusively to their own residents. Since this company could not develop the project, it was taken over by another company, which changed the location of the project's main infrastructure from the first to the second village, much to the dismay of the first village, which lost the jobs initially planned for the construction and operation of this infrastructure. Not surprisingly, the second village insisted on exclusively employing its residents. The first village, as expected, contested the relocation of the infrastructure to retain the jobs. The tug-of-war between the two villages resulted in acts of violence and disruptions to the activities of this new company, which had based the site change on objective elements related to the project's profitability. The lessons learned from this situation, which would have been ironic if it did not involve villagers' lives and had not led to violence, can be applied at the municipal, prefectural, and regional levels.

In response to a patriarch who vehemently argued for the necessity that his prefecture receives a larger contribution to local development since it hosted the mine, I explained to him that he should avoid discussing this topic in public because, in a few years, the mining site would be relocated from his prefecture to another, due to the depletion of the deposit. His sudden, bewildering, and definitive silence almost triggered laughter on my part, which I managed to stifle out of respect for this man of a certain age who, despite his strong and overwhelming passionate voice, displayed impressive lucidity.

Beyond these confusions, which can sometimes have dramatic consequences, especially in the relations between local communities and mining companies on one hand, and between different communities on the other hand, a meticulous analysis of local content in terms of procurements from Guinean companies reveals nuances that can be important in evaluating the economic impact of mining activities. Indeed, awarding a contract to an international company established and registered in Guinea, without being counted in the local content quota, can sometimes have a better impact on local content than a company owned by Guineans. If this international company predominantly employs Guineans and buys its raw materials locally from Guinean economic actors, it can create more wealth in Guinea than a company owned by Guineans that predominantly employs expatriates and imports most of its raw materials. This possibility that, in some cases, local content is more significant in the international company, or that "non-local" content is more significant in the Guinean company, calls for more vigilance for a more nuanced analysis of the effective local content share, beyond compliance with legal quotas. Appearances can be deceiving. Therefore, it is important to ensure that local content is not just " local container."

Furthermore, the promotion of local content should be done in a spirit of solidarity among communities, with the perspective of the temporary nature of any mining operation, calling not only to strengthen traditional economic activities but also to show hospitality towards Guineans from other origins who might be hosts to members of the host community in the future. This is important to ensure that mining activities serve more as a factor for mixing between different communities than a factor of division, conflicts, or simply social and economic balkanization of the country.

The interest shown by all social and economic actors in local content is commensurate with the role of this significant aspect of the mining sector's development policy. The promotion of local content is a powerful instrument in favor of the mining industry's contribution to economic diversification and poverty reduction. Not to mention its potential effects on social cohesion and peace. It facilitates the effective participation of Guineans in the nation's economic life, thus contributing to their social and economic well-being. Through local purchases, it contributes to the sharing of mining wealth while offsetting the relatively low level of job creation in the mining industry. It helps strengthen the technical and financial capacities of the workforce and businesses, which can use these capabilities in other socioeconomic sectors in Guinea and export them. Construction companies in Guinea, having benefited from the requirements of mining companies to improve and achieve a better financial position, are now building public infrastructure in Guinea and sometimes abroad. Mining, through local content, contributes to lifting the Guinean economy; as evidenced by the 8,031 billion Guinean francs (over 900 million US dollars)[35] in subcontracting contracts obtained by Guinean SMEs in the sector between 2011 and 2019.

[35] MNH Consulting, Impact study of the mining sector on the national economy ("Etude d'impact du secteur minier sur l'économie nationale"). 2020

19

Local content: the need for a collective approach

To ensure that the contribution of the mining industry, through the promotion of local content, meets the country's expectations, it is necessary for all stakeholders to fully play their roles.

The state has adopted a national policy on local content, a sectoral policy on local content in mining, as well as specific provisions regarding local content. Additionally, the Ministry of Mines and Geology conducted an evaluation, by an independent international firm, from February to June 2017, of the promotion of local content within eight mining companies in the bauxite and gold sectors that were either in the construction or operational phase. This assessment, one of the first in Africa, focused on the practices and performances of mining companies in operation or in advanced development. The firm evaluated the companies involved in terms of employment, training, and procurement, based on information primarily collected from the mining companies and other relevant entities. This evaluation highlighted the following key points:

- Overall results were insufficient or average.

- Regarding local employment, among the eight sampled companies, only one was clearly in compliance with the Mining Code quotas.
- Concerning local procurement, only one company reported having a well-established local procurement plan, and in terms of performance, three companies showed average results.
- Overall, only one company demonstrated relatively commendable practices and performances.

Following the evaluation, feedback was provided to the companies, and monitoring was carried out by the Ministry of Mines and other departments. Beyond the observations, this exercise has created a greater awareness among the companies and fostered healthy competition among them.

Thanks to the promotion of local content in the mines, many local businesses from other sectors now benefit from the spin-offs of mining activities. These include catering and food supply services; construction; environmental and geological services; professional services—financial, legal, and human resources; the supply of construction materials; logistics, distribution, and transportation services; maintenance and mechanical repair services; the supply of personal protective equipment; spare parts, machinery, and the sale/rental of vehicles; health, safety, and environmental (HSE) training; and hospitality.

This demonstrates the positive ripple effects of the mining industry on the broader local economy.

These eleven sectors have been identified as having high potential in the study conducted by the American firm DAI Energy and Resources Group for the Ministry of Mines, with the support of the International Finance

Corporation (IFC)[36], between June and September 2017, assessing the level of promotion of local content and its growth potential in the mining industry. This study highlights the potential and challenges in terms of local content in the industry. It was conducted with eight mining companies and 138 local SMEs. While the hospitality, logistics, distribution, and transportation sectors, as well as HSE training, are considered relatively competitive, the same cannot be said for catering and food supply services, as well as environmental and geological services.

The estimates from this study indicate that Guinean SMEs could capture, in the long term, approximately 8.8 billion US dollars in contract opportunities in the mining industry, accounting for around 441 to 588 million US dollars in annual turnover.

Regarding the labor aspect of local content, it was already estimated, including indirect jobs, that the mining companies in the sample generate approximately 100,000 jobs in total, including indirect and induced jobs. At the time of the study, 94% of direct jobs were held by Guineans, contrary to any misinformation that might circulate about the overall level of employment of Guineans in the mines.

Furthermore, the study results show that "each of the 53 professions identified as key to the operation of the eleven sectors has established training programs in Guinea. Each year, around 15,000 students graduate in these 53 professions, some of whom will work for the mining industry. However, the number of graduates in some fields is not sufficient for the needs of the mining industry, such as heavy equipment operators and hotel staff."

---

[36] DAI Energy and Resources Group. "Assessment of the Level of Local Content Promotion and its Growth Potential in the Mining Sector." 2017

The main challenges identified were insufficient knowledge and experience in the mining industry, lack of information about opportunities in the mines, financial capacity constraints, and insufficient qualifications in the workforce.

The results of this study, highlighting deficiencies at various levels in promoting local content, have been widely disseminated by the Ministry of Mines and used to drive reforms in the sector, including the implementation of the action plan proposed at the end of the study.

In contrast to my initial months at the ministry, from 2017 onward, we observed a decrease in visits from local entrepreneurs complaining about the lack of business opportunities in mining. This was probably because, on the one hand, we encouraged them to contact companies directly without any possibility of my recommendations, and on the other hand, many of them had likely secured contracts in ongoing mining projects and operations. Nevertheless, I regret that it has always been challenging to obtain information from local entrepreneurs, perhaps due to a habit of keeping their activities discreet, regarding the benefits they derive from the implementation of the local content policy. Conversely, unsurprisingly, those who do not secure contracts have always been quick to complain, even when they do not adhere to the required procedures. With very few exceptions, I could only gauge the real effects of the government's and companies' actions through information from mining companies.

The evaluations of local content promotion have been part of the identification of opportunities and challenges, as well as monitoring the implementation of regulations, which we hope to conduct periodically beyond the current quarterly monitoring. This monitoring and control, which are the responsibility of the state, require permanent resources and close inter-ministerial collaboration. Further strengthening the regulatory framework and capacities is necessary to achieve full effectiveness on this front. Control should also include periodic social audits of mining companies by the General Labor Inspection to ensure that contractual and working conditions comply with existing regulations. It would complement audits on the training and development program and "*Guineanization*" in accordance with the quotas required by the Mining Code.

Concerning access to local purchases, the Mining Code requires each mining titleholder to submit an annual report on its use of SMEs, SMIs, and businesses owned or controlled by Guineans, as well as its activities aimed at creating or strengthening Guinean capacities.

The government should continue its efforts to enhance the competitiveness of local businesses, especially by focusing on capacity building, facilitating access to credit, and reducing additional costs associated with tax discrepancies. The last point deserves particular attention, especially concerning Value Added Tax (VAT) and customs tax exemptions. Local companies tend to have structurally higher costs in their offers compared to foreign companies, all other factors being equal. This is because foreign companies benefit from exemptions granted in mining agreements due to their status as direct subcontractors with no other activities in Guinea. To address this issue, we initiated a scheme in which a local company could establish a project-specific company for each contract, effectively becoming the exclusive direct subcontractor to the mining company. This helps the local company meet the exemption criteria. However, for this scheme to work effectively, the mining company should recognize the transfer of capabilities from the local parent company to the project-specific company to ensure that the latter is not disadvantaged during the bid evaluation process.

Furthermore, work permits should be issued by the Guinean Employment Promotion Agency "with the advice of the mining administration," in accordance with Article 108 of the Mining Code. Strict enforcement of this article could bring a significant change in the effectiveness of the localization policy, especially for positions of responsibility within mining companies. A systematic review of expatriate recruitment by the Ministry of Mines during the COVID-19 pandemic showed that companies sometimes opt for the easy route by simply transferring foreign experts from one mine in another country to Guinea. For example, a mining company that wanted to replace its Guinean general manager with an expatriate was pleasantly surprised that by using international headhunting firms, they had a wide selection of candidates to choose from. This competitive and international procedure, implemented by the company following our insistence on having the position filled by a Guinean rather than a foreigner (to prevent regression in the company's localization process), resulted in a substantial number of eligible candidates for the position. From this experience of sourcing Guinean candidates through competitive means both in Guinea and abroad, following a previous effort in 2016, we obtained proof that, if needed, the good faith of companies can yield results in line with their own competitive selection criteria and processes, without interference from the government.

In addition to the government's strict oversight, the success of this policy promoting Guineans within companies depends on complementary state investments in training, especially technical and vocational education, to supply the labor force that companies require. Efforts in this area in recent years have been moving in the right direction. This includes adapting the supply of education to the demands of mining companies by having company representation on the boards of educational institutions. It also involves the construction of six regional vocational schools (ERAM) in the prefectures of Boké, Coyah, Dabola, Labé, N'Zérékoré, and Siguiri, with four of them already completed, and six other vocational schools in progress. The operationalization of all these ERAMs will contribute to creating the skills that mining companies need to ensure the development of their activities while employing more Guineans.

With the support of technical and financial partners, notably the International Finance Corporation (IFC) of the World Bank Group, the government took initiatives to implement the policy of promoting local content in the mining industry, in addition to those carried out within the framework of the national policy by the ministries responsible for SMEs and private investment. To this end, the Suppliers Subcontracting and partnership Marketplace (BSTP) was established in November 2018. This initiative aims to address the information gap for SMEs regarding market opportunities, provide a platform for connecting SMEs with mining companies, and strengthen the capacities and access to financing for SMEs, enabling them to meet the requirements of these companies.

The BSTP already records encouraging results with a board of directors dominated by the private sector and a young and dynamic management team. More than 1,800 SMEs are registered there. Over 3,000 SME managers have received capacity-building from the BSTP. Also, more than 150 tenders have been published on the platform, of which more than 80 were won by companies registered with the BSTP (equivalent to more than 45 million US dollars in contracts). This highlights the usefulness of this platform for member SMEs, who have already benefited from over 12 million US dollars in facilities from commercial banks through the BSTP.

The initiative to create the Suppliers Subcontracting and partnership Marketplace (BSTP), undertaken by the State as part of the national policy to promote local content, has been implemented by the Ministry of Mines, in coordination with the ministries responsible for private investment and SMEs, with a focus on effective ownership by the private sector. The form of "public utility" association, rather than a public body, the independent governance and financing mode, and the emphasis on private sector involvement in governance, along with the consistent commitment of the State and IFC alongside the BSTP, are elements that give hope for the sustainability of this unprecedented system in this form in Africa and is already inspiring other countries.

If the role of the State is fundamental in implementing the local content promotion policy, that of mining companies is even more critical as entities that generate employment and business opportunities. The adoption of policies related to Corporate Social Responsibility and the promotion of local content in the mines (in April 2017), as well as the current regulations, provide them with the framework for implementing local content requirements. Moreover, many companies have internal policies that largely cover the state's requirements. However, it is not uncommon to find that some officials and agents responsible for promoting local content within mining companies are more concerned with ticking boxes related to meeting criteria than with the actual impact of the company's actions on the level of local content achieved. The fundamental mistake would be to consider the promotion of Guineans and Guinean businesses as a mere professional obligation, as a simple humanitarian action, to acquire the famous social license to operate, referring to the approval and support of all local stakeholders towards the company for fulfilling its social responsibility and commitments to local communities. Beyond the social license, sincere and responsible promotion of local content is a medium and long-term commercial and financial imperative. The economy generated by using locally available, less costly skills meets this imperative. Additionally, support from local communities and resulting population goodwill generally helps significantly reduce conflicts with communities, avoiding the company's loss of time and resources invested in resolving these conflicts, as well as the loss resulting from decreases or stoppages of activities. Finally, wealth redistribution through local employment or purchases significantly contributes to reducing social pressure, especially in terms of jobs, on the relatively job-poor mining activity.

Despite all these objective advantages for the organization that is the mining company, individuals within the company, including Guineans, may sometimes succumb to personal interests or the moral comfort of placing a friend or a colleague from school at a particular position or biasing the subcontractor selection process in favor of a supplier with whom they have business or personal ties. These collusions, which are not uncommon in the mining industry, create situations of injustice that tarnish the image of companies and the sector.

The other source of bias lies in the pursuit of economies of scale by large international groups, which, through their purchasing departments, prefer to negotiate contracts globally for all their subsidiaries. This practice is common among multinational corporations that purchase large aggregated volumes (for their subsidiaries), giving them negotiating power over suppliers and allowing them to drive prices down. These purchases from international suppliers by these multinationals, sometimes for nonsophisticated products, then result in significant missed opportunities for local companies. The same applies to the sending of expatriates to Guinea from the company's sites in other countries, simply for convenience or ease, as forming a new team requires more effort and risk. A company that discreetly sent a group of drivers from one of its subsidiaries in a neighboring country quickly reconsidered after a warning from the ministry and dissatisfaction within the local community. A driver training program implemented for this purpose proved, not surprisingly, more beneficial for both the company and the community, with drivers receiving a local salary, despite the cost of the training.

Mining companies, while maintaining minimum requirements in terms of health, safety, environment, and technical standards, must adopt an objective but flexible approach in seeking local skills and partnerships with local companies. The genuine commitment of companies to promoting local content must consider the difficulties faced by local businesses. One of the main challenges for SMEs is access to financing. Some mining companies, in collaboration with local banks, have succeeded in implementing a financing guarantee scheme based on contracts signed with mining companies. Not strictly requiring financial capacities upfront, while having the required risk coverage, can open more business opportunities for local SMEs. The effective operationalization of the leasing system should also help facilitate access to financing. However, this is only possible if commercial banks are willing to apply the guarantee system corresponding to the traditional leasing scheme. In reality, banks tend not to be satisfied with the equipment covered by the lease as collateral, contrary to the basic principle of this financing mechanism. The basic principle of leasing should be applied, even if a stronger system to secure equipment against diversion or theft is included in the scheme. Additionally, a monitoring and training support plan for SMEs, as required in the Mining Code, can have a real impact on their development without being overly costly. This plan can be designed and implemented in collaboration with national or international institutions, some of which may even contribute to financing the plan.

In any case, employees of companies and the companies themselves must understand that the only path to a sustainable, peaceful, and healthy coexistence with local populations necessarily involves sincere and proactive commitment and actions in promoting local content. This is essential for establishing an equitable relationship with these populations and the respective states. Because any relationship that is not equitable is not viable.

In this promotion of local content, local entrepreneurs and job seekers also have a role to play. In addition to the support they receive, they should strive to improve their skills to ensure competitiveness in recruitment and contract allocation processes. In the era of information technology, they often have access to a wealth of information that can enhance their capabilities. Some may cite the cost of internet access as a barrier to self-learning. During a conference with students at a local university, I observed that at least 95% of the students in the audience had internet access on their smartphones, even though they had just told me that the government should help them access the internet! While it is true that the government should play its role in ensuring affordable access, the key lies in attitude. It should not be about waiting for assistance from third parties or the government before acting, but rather about utilizing everything available at hand before seeking external assistance.

Local businesses and job seekers must seize every opportunity and even invest to become more competitive. The only way to retain and thrive in these opportunities is by delivering at least the expected results for the company, which needs them for survival in an environment where it also faces competition in the market. Instead of pursuing competitiveness, many individuals choose to invest more in influence peddling than in upgrading their personal or business skills to access opportunities. This represents a significant obstacle to the fair promotion of local content.

The state is often criticized for not adequately promoting local content in the mines. While it is good for local businesses to have subcontracting opportunities with mining companies, it is even better for them to become mining companies themselves. This is the ultimate level of promoting local content. In this regard, a review in November 2020 showed that Guineans, in comparison to other nationalities, own shares or control (over 50%) the majority of mining permits (primarily for exploration) in the mining sector. Guineans are shareholders in 43% of mining permits and majority owners in 29% of these permits. Specifically, they are shareholders in 59% and majority owners in 33% of bauxite permits. In the gold field, Guineans are shareholders in 44% and majority owners in 27% of permits. These figures refute the belief that Guineans are insufficiently involved in mining activities. As the most nationalist among us desire, the Guinean private sector has all the opportunities to control the development of mining projects in Guinea. Why is this not effective? In fact, many Guineans active in the mines are content with having their day-to-day expenses covered by their partners and sometimes even living an unduly lavish life at their partners' expense. Partners who realize that their funds, which they bring for project development, are being squandered eventually withdraw from the project, which subsequently falls apart. Guineans without means eventually lose their permits and repeat the cycle later by finding another partner whom they use as a cash cow. An eternal cycle with no projects coming to fruition. I was unpleasantly surprised by several Guinean intermediaries who fought against our decision to ensure that Guineans have a larger share (at least one-third) in quarries, preferring a meager commission of a few thousand dollars at most to meet their immediate needs.

The few Guineans who succeed are those who behave responsibly with their partners and/or decide to take risks by investing a portion of the funds for research. Even among these, many withdraw too quickly from the project, with at best a tiny share of the final project, prioritizing immediate financial compensation. However, the more advanced the project with an exploitable deposit (in its research or feasibility study phase), the more valuable it becomes. A few rare Guineans, however, have had the intelligence, patience, and means to retain a strong minority share or control in the mining companies they have created. These cases, unfortunately rare, represent the Holy Grail in terms of local content. Guineans benefit from subcontracting contracts, others from jobs, and the Guinean owner from dividends. As early as 2016, we approached large local SMEs in the construction industry, whose profession is the gateway to mining, to encourage them to take an interest in the mining sector. Few responded to our call, which was insistent during the following years.

Beyond what the state, technical partners, and mining companies can do, the real challenge for local businesses in accessing markets is the awareness of the need to develop the capabilities that allow them to meet the requirements of these companies. For this, a certain level of professional maturity, especially in terms of organizational quality, and a certain level of awareness are required within a medium and long-term framework, rather than just opportunistic short-term approaches. Companies, individually and through their associations, must better organize themselves, particularly through the establishment of access to training platforms, pooling resources, and collective approaches in large-scale contracts. Local businesses, through their individual and collective organization and their medium to long-term vision, must effectively seize the opportunities around mining operations. Studies, often carried out with the support of technical and financial partners, such as those with the IFC on subcontracting opportunities and the regional development strategy of Boké, provide sources for identifying opportunities that do not necessarily require extraordinary financial resources.

20

Local socio-economic impact of the sector through FODEL and FNDL

In addition to local content opportunities, the economic contribution of the mining industry extends to community project development opportunities through the Local Economic Development Fund (FODEL) and the National Fund for Local Development (FNDL).

The Local Economic Development Fund (FODEL) is funded by the local development contribution, which represents 0.5% to 1% of the mining companies' turnover, paid directly at the community level, in accordance with the provisions of Article 130 of the Mining Code. FODEL is a contribution owed by mining companies to offset the impact of their activities and, thus, ensure harmony between the affected communities and these companies, which, through this local contribution, directly contribute to the socio-economic development of these communities.

The National Fund for Local Development (FNDL), implemented by the National Agency for Local Government Financing (ANAFIC), is one of the significant innovations of the 2011 Mining Code (amended in 2013). FNDL complements FODEL to prevent inequality in local development between mining areas and those without active mines. FNDL involves the allocation of 15% of certain mining taxes collected in the national development budget and transferred by the state for the benefit of all local authorities, in accordance with Article 165 of the Mining Code.

These two mechanisms contribute to addressing one of the most significant challenges facing the mining industry: the sustainable management of economic, social, and environmental impacts. Beyond the policies of corporate social responsibility and local content, the operational framework ensuring the responsible exploitation of mineral resources is gradually being established.

Under the Local Economic Development Fund (FODEL), more than 292 billion Guinean francs (more than 30 million US dollars) were mobilized from 2015 to 2020 in various mining areas. This has enabled the financing of over 1,400 local development projects, including 1,200 income-generating projects for young people and women, potentially creating more than 25,000 jobs.

Furthermore, the effective allocation of a portion of the mining revenues stipulated in the code by the state to local communities in 2019, through the National Fund for Local Development (FNDL), enabled the financing of annual investment plans to the tune of 463 billion Guinean francs (50 million US Dollars), benefiting nearly 800 projects across the country.

In addition to the impact of the initiatives already launched, it is important to note that the resources of FODEL and FNDL are annual. Under the Local Economic Development Fund (FODEL), if the current momentum is maintained, mining localities should receive 125 billion Guinean francs (13 million US dollars) per year from 2025, then 200 billion Guinean francs (20 million US dollars) per year in 2030. The financing of communities through ANAFIC, under the National Fund Local Development (FNDL), should reach 700 billion Guinean francs (more than 70 million US dollars) per year in 2025 and then exceed 1 trillion Guinean francs (US$100 million) per year in 2030.

This regularity and the increasing volume of allocations from these two funds will allow local communities to have significant resources for the regular financing of their local projects and ensure an irreversible momentum toward their development.

I have a strong belief that the success of these two initiatives in the long run will significantly contribute to improving the quality of local governance within communities, which is currently the greatest challenge for achieving their impact in the short and medium terms. The ongoing opportunity to implement projects that contribute to a qualitative change in the living conditions of the populations could increasingly attract young qualified professionals and experienced senior executives towards local management, creating a form of urban exodus. This exodus may involve young individuals seeking project opportunities to implement.

This hope, however, can quickly transform into a development reality only if the annual evaluation of the initiatives is carried out rigorously, with the implementation of all possible sanctions resulting from audit or evaluation results. Success also depends on the effective compliance of the implementation with the following three basic principles:

- Inclusive, rigorous, and equitable management of the funds for the exclusive benefit of the beneficiary populations.
- The strict adherence to absolute transparency in the management of the funds, especially towards the beneficiary populations.

- The effective consideration of activities aimed at empowering women and youth.

Another indirect impact of FODEL and FNDL should be the progressive improvement in the quality of local executives. Delinquent municipal councils will likely face public backlash during electoral terms, which will be of greater interest to the populations due to the possibility of implementing more ambitious action plans and well-funded, regularly replenished budgets. With increased interest in local government from individuals experienced in management (whether in the public or private sector), it would not be surprising to witness more municipal councils equipped with management capabilities far exceeding the current standards.

In addition to their involvement in the selection and financing of projects, particularly for youth and women, the populations are the main link to the success of the Local Economic Development Fund (FODEL) and the National Fund Local Development (FNDL). For this to happen, strong community involvement is needed in the development of Local Development Plans and Annual Investment Programs, as well as active NGO and citizen oversight of fund management.

21

Local processing of mining production

The issue of local processing of mining products is a major concern for the government, as well as for people of all ages and backgrounds in Guinea. The legitimacy of this concern can be summarized by a simple observation: all the countries that have successfully used mining to drive industrialization have gone through the local processing of their production. This has led to a structural transformation of their countries, particularly through increased value added to the economy, the development of human capital, and multiplier effects on other fields of the economy (such as infrastructure and energy). Guinea should undoubtedly follow this rule as well. The desire to locally process our production has been a fundamental aspect of the country's mining policy since its independence, and even before independence if we consider initiatives taken by the colonial power in this direction. In this context, the Friguia plant was established in 1959 in partnership with the French company Pechiney. As the first alumina plant on African soil, this factory was intended to be followed by other processing projects, particularly with the effective development of the hydroelectric potential of the Konkouré River.

Despite this stated will at all levels, the country has not set up other processing units for its mining production. Was it because it no longer had mining resources to sustain new units? Or was it due to a lack of will from the leaders afterward? Or perhaps, faced with the absence of a market to justify the construction of new units? The obvious answer to all these questions is "no."

So, why haven't there been any new factories?

Answering this question should interest any socio-economic or political leader. Unfortunately, the issue of local processing, however serious it may be, has become a populist topic in public debate, with an approach that suggests that all it takes is for a government to make a wish for transformation to happen swiftly. It is precisely to address this question that a new policy for the development of the mines has been put in place over the years to achieve this legitimate and, above all, necessary goal for our industrialization.

Why haven't there been any new processing units after Friguia? Without wanting to revisit history since independence, one can simply say that the conditions were not met for a long time. The first condition is the presence of an investment framework that allows an investor to make a significant investment (such is the case with transformation) in a country like Guinea, which also lacks sufficient energy production, qualified labor, and local production of the inputs necessary for the transformation process.

In terms of scale, an alumina plant in such an environment requires an investment of around a billion dollars. From 1958 to 2010, no individual private investment exceeded $200 million. Questioned about this fact, and despite a relatively long presence in Guinea, an investor who was active in the 2000s responded, "Guinea is not a country where you can invest a billion dollars."

While I reserve the right not to agree with this statement and even feel wounded in my pride, like any other Guinean, one fact remains unchanged: it painfully but factually reveals the level of risk perception (or investment level) that a mining industry investor was willing or unwilling to expose themselves to in Guinea at that time. With the State, given its limited resources, unable to provide recourse for such an investment, it goes without saying that this simply would not have happened without a more favorable investment climate.

For an investor to mobilize the resources to develop a business project, they must have the assurance that the investment framework allows them to generate sufficient revenues to recover their invested equity, repay the loans they have taken, and realize the expected profit, which is their main motivation for investing. A mining project typically spans a long duration (often several years of study and over a decade of operation), so the investor seeks long-term assurance. The quality of institutions that ensure the survival of agreements across regimes and the adherence to the terms of agreements by each regime is, therefore, critical for the investment decision-making process. The exceptional quality of deposits is not always sufficient. Moreover, the investor is exposed to market fluctuations, which are beyond the control of the State.

In a business environment that does not guarantee fair treatment, commitment fulfillment, or the avoidance of arbitrary actions, the "investors" who appear are typically those who lack the necessary resources, credibility to mobilize substantial investments and, more importantly, those who make every effort to achieve their return on investment as quickly as possible and by any means. This is also applicable to investment decisions related to raw production.

Since 2011, there has been, first and foremost, the streamlining of the legal and regulatory framework with the adoption of the new Mining Code, which, contrary to some claims, has attracted significant investments from demanding sources. Subsequently, there were reforms in the organization and functioning of the state in the mining sector, particularly in terms of efficiency, transparency, and adherence to the approval procedure for agreements (ministries, Council of Ministers, National Assembly, Constitutional Court). The system as a whole now provides investors with much more confidence that rights are acquired under normal conditions and will be preserved as long as they fulfill their obligations. The completed and ongoing reforms have apparently provided enough assurance to investors to consider Guinea as a country where one can invest a billion dollars... or more! Indeed, several projects exceeding this investment amount are in progress or completed and operational, including the GAC project, the CBG project (in its two phases), and the SMB project.

In addition to the level of investment, another fundamental question in the transformation is that of energy. If the energy produced by the Konkouré River was to be used in the transformation process, the complete realization of the dams in the Konkouré system (Garafiri, Kaleta, Souapiti, and Amaria) would not be enough to cover all of Guinea's transformation needs. At best, they would cover the needs of some of the five new alumina refinery projects initiated since 2011, in addition to the four initiated by previous regimes. Accelerating gas exploration and seeking a competitive and viable source of gas or other energy supplies are the avenues explored to meet the transformation needs that could lead to massive industrialization in the mines.

In the short term, the question of the thermal energy source required for refineries remains essential and urgent. The government must make a choice that considers the economic viability of the projects and the environmental impact of the chosen energy source. The choice depends on the viability of the projects in the case of choosing gas («cleaner») or the level of pollution in the case of a possible choice of coal, which is an option considered by some companies in ongoing feasibility studies. Is gas competitive enough to ensure the economic viability of alumina refinery projects? Can current technologies reduce coal pollution to an acceptable level while many countries abandon this energy source? What would be the potentially acceptable level of pollution (acceptable standards) at a time when the country is engaged in the global fight against climate change? To address all these questions, the ministry has hired a specialized firm to provide an objective decision-making basis to the government, considering environmental and economic imperatives in the development of alumina plant projects.

The other topic that is often debated is the export of raw material without engaging in transformation. Some argue that raw production is excessive. In fact, no Guinean government has previously decided to reduce bauxite production, as the debate generally revolves around this substance. On the contrary, governments that have succeeded since Independence have all made efforts to increase bauxite production. Unfortunately, the conditions for exponential growth were not met for a long time, as bauxite exploitation requires heavy investments in transport and evacuation infrastructure that in the past required involvement and even financing from the state. In this regard, I would like to emphasize that all the infrastructure under construction is financed by private investors, without any financial contribution or guarantee from the state.

The natural goal of increasing production finally began to materialize in 2015, after several years of reforms. Moving from the 7th to the 2nd position as a global bauxite producer, surpassing Brazil and China but still behind Australia, in less than five years, is indeed an achievement to be appreciated. It positions Guinea as a key player in the industry, with an increasingly favorable position for its mining development, including local processing. Furthermore, the resources derived from Guinea's exports enable the country to continue improving its investment climate, especially by investing in infrastructure, thereby facilitating the realization of local processing projects. This strategy also allows the state to secure essential resources for building basic infrastructure in vital sectors for the country's socio-economic development, such as education, healthcare, etc. Similarly, these revenues can contribute to the construction of roads and other essential infrastructure for the development of key sectors like agriculture.

The continued increase in annual bauxite production, while not incompatible with local processing, is therefore justified and sustainable in the long term. Other countries, less endowed but more developed and recognized for their successes in socio-economic development, have long produced and exported more bauxite than Guinea. Indonesia, which had banned the export of raw bauxite in 2014, reversed this decision and resumed its exports with renewed vigor.

Moreover, even by producing, for example, 100 million tonnes of bauxite per year, Guinea could produce competitively high-quality bauxite for 400 years. The production and export of raw bauxite are justified not only by Guinea's need to finance its short, medium, and long-term development but also by the risk of replacing bauxite with another substance for alumina production. Alumina can, for example, be extracted from clay. The market opportunity is not permanent; it depends on technological advancements and the possibility of commercial replacement production. Guinea must seize the opportunity it has to finance its development, create jobs, and generate wealth, within the framework of responsible mineral resource exploitation and environmental respect.

The investments made possible by current and future mining revenues, along with the development of shared transportation and energy infrastructure in ongoing integrated mining projects, represent the best way to equip Guinea with capacities that make it less dependent on mines over the years. This is in an increasingly diversified, prosperous, and inclusive economy.

The goal is not just to leave an extraordinary potential for future generations; it is to pass on prosperity and development within a framework of good governance, which includes effectively mobilizing resources and using them rationally.

At first glance, local processing offers more advantages in terms of employment, income, industrialization, and environmental impact. However, to fully benefit from this local processing, special attention will need to be given to the changes it will bring about in terms of creating new, more sophisticated jobs, new logistical and commercial chains, new challenges in managing industrial waste, and more. Vocational and higher education, support for SMEs, and several other government interventions should incorporate these new challenges, transforming them into real opportunities.

In the debate about local processing, it is important to carefully examine the expectations that local processing will automatically solve the problems of unemployment and state revenue. There is no doubt that it is better to process bauxite to create more local added value and higher-quality jobs. However, it must be borne in mind that modern refineries employ fewer and fewer people due to the increasing automation of the production chain. Between 1,500 to 2,000 employees work in a refinery producing one to two million tonnes, which, in terms of employment, falls far short of the country's needs to significantly reduce unemployment. Additionally, Guinea cannot build an infinite number of refineries. It must first ensure that the commitments in progress are realized (a little less than ten refineries) and work towards the gradual relocation of refineries supplied by Guinean bauxite. The state must absolutely ensure that the commitments related to the construction of refineries are respected and that their operation is facilitated to encourage more investments in local processing. Indeed, the relocation of refineries to Guinea, while financially beneficial to the companies, can be effectively realized only if the country creates competitive conditions for access to qualified labor, inputs, and energy. A coercive approach (through commitments in agreements) must be combined with an incentive approach to attract additional investments in the context of relocating bauxite processing to Guinea. Abrupt decisions, not considering investment constraints, do not necessarily produce the desired effects. In short, the shift towards processing must be made with determination, but also with the efforts required to improve the investment environment. Extreme positions that ignore investment conditions will not achieve the intended objectives. For example, an abrupt halt to bauxite exports would not be realistic. It would even put at risk the achievement of the objective of local processing. Investors in the crude bauxite exploitation have begun to have a certain understanding of the environment and a certain confidence that allows them to commit the significant amounts required for investment in processing. A cap on exports for mining companies not engaged in processing is, in fact, already in place.

Finally, the assumption that the state would de facto earn more revenue with local processing is not always true. In the current situation (especially in terms of labor, access to inputs, energy, and infrastructure, freight costs), all investors demand tax concessions that reduce state revenue, at least during the early years of production. These concessions are justified by the need for private companies to make investments outside the processing unit itself, necessitating compensation for the increased overall investment compared to other countries. Besides the taxes and fees subject to exemptions (temporary or permanent), dividends are another potential source of revenue for the state. The low level of participation envisaged, for example, in the Mining Code for a refinery (5 or 7.5%), to attract investment, does not allow for substantial dividend income. Moreover, for such large private investments, the initial years are deficit years, and therefore without dividends. If the state wants to generate substantial income, it must invest in processing itself to reach participation levels that allow it to generate significant dividends that will be added to taxes and fees after the exemption years. This practice of investing public resources in large commercial projects contradicts the liberal economic policy initiated by the state since 1985. However, it can be justified in some cases by strategic necessity and can be executed through state commercial entities without affecting the national development budget, which focuses on non-commercial investment. The current production of raw bauxite creates the possibility for the state to access the financial resources to carry out such an investment. One option is a public-private partnership, either directly with private partners or through a commercial partnership with them to process their production and/or supply their aluminum plant. Aware of the opportunities and constraints related to local bauxite processing, we launched the revival of the study for the construction of a refinery with CBG in 2018. In my opinion, this project is currently one of the best refinery projects for the Guinean state. On the one hand, because by holding 49% of CBG's shares, the State would have access to a substantial share of the dividends generated by the refinery, unlike other projects. On the other hand, because CBG is already managed by Guinean employees, technology transfer to the nationals would occur automatically without the need for a new mechanism that might require additional efforts from the various parties.

Furthermore, in this case, the State would have the strategic option to process the production of other companies in a refinery it initiates, either alone or more likely in partnership, benefiting and providing private shareholders with the economies of scale that this can generate. The major challenge remains the financing of such a refinery, but with annual revenues that could reach one billion dollars in the next 5-7 years, the State will have a financial lever that allows it to participate in financing significant investments directly or indirectly.

In any case, local processing requires a level of governance quality, capacity, investment, and experience that the current phase of exporting raw products can provide to Guinea, provided it is utilized with rigor, responsibility, and determination.

The Guinean government now possesses enhanced capabilities due to training and field experience. Reforms have facilitated the attraction and implementation of significant investments, the understanding of the global market improves year by year, and refinery projects (including four with completed feasibility studies) are receiving more diligent attention. The country's energy production capacity is significantly improving, and technical education schools are in the process of becoming operational. All these advancements, which need to be continued, are gradually and surely paving the way for the realization of the local processing phase, which extends beyond bauxite to encompass other resources like gold and iron.

Furthermore, the investments made in bauxite have set the stage for more favorable conditions for alumina transformation soon. Beyond the actual investments, there is a geostrategic significance for Guinea in becoming a major player in the bauxite market to accelerate alumina development projects. Guinea's voice carries weight in the market today and can better engage with investors and the market at large to transition to local processing. The recent substantial increase in maritime freight costs and the progressive sophistication of the Chinese economy are also factors that favor the establishment of new alumina plants in Guinea. The prospects are promising if the momentum of improving the investment framework and closely monitoring projects continues diligently.

22

Very promising prospects for the sector if…

What should the Guinea's mines look like in five years, in ten years? Providing a definitive answer to this question would be akin to having a crystal ball. However, based on the reforms already implemented and the parameters of ongoing projects, we can take the risk of making reasonable projections.

The essential prerequisites for achieving the objectives outlined in these projections are stability and peace in the country, the continued pursuit of the governance improvement agenda in the sector, and the overall maintenance of global market prospects. The realization of these conditions would enable Guinea to continue the development momentum of the mines towards the attainment of the goals of ongoing development projects. Based on this, we can reasonably estimate that the sector will experience the following developments in the next decade:

- The effective realization of investments commitments acquired between 2010 and 2020, totaling at least 25 billion US dollars by 2030.
- Significant progress towards diversifying its mining production. In addition to bauxite, gold, diamonds, and alumina currently in production, the country should

commence commercial production of iron and graphite before 2025, as well as heavy metals such as zircon and ilmenite, used in various industries, including aerospace.

- The number of companies in production should increase from 16 to over 20 by 2025, and to more than 25 by 2030, compared to only 6 companies in production in 2010.
- Bauxite production should increase from 70 million tonnes in 2019 to over 100 million tonnes by 2025. Alumina production should increase from a capacity of 600,000 to 1.6 million tonnes in 2025, and to over 4.5 million tonnes by 2030, with the launch of at least three new refineries.
- Industrial and semi-industrial gold production should increase from 13 tonnes in 2019 to over 18 tonnes by 2025, with the launch of three new mines.
- Iron production should exceed 50 million tonnes by 2030, with the launch of at least two new productions.
- Mining revenues should increase from 435 million US dollars in 2018 to a stable level of over 600 million US dollars by 2025, and to at least one billion US dollars by 2030.
- Direct and indirect jobs created in the mines should increase from 50,000 to 100,000 by 2025, and to 150,000 by 2030.
- Local community financing through ANAFIC, under the National Fund for Local Development (FNDL), should reach 700 billion Guinean francs (approximately 80 million US dollars) per year by 2025, and exceed 1,000 billion Guinean francs (around 110 million US Dollars) per year by 2030.
- Under the Local Economic Development Fund (FODEL), mining localities should receive 125 billion Guinean francs per year from 2025 (around 14 million US

dollars), and 200 billion Guinean francs per year by 2030 (more than 22 million US dollars).

Beautiful and even idyllic picture, isn't it? Hopefully, it remains achievable, provided that Guinea experiences a good period of peace and stability, that the governance of the mines continues to improve, with better collection and better use of revenues in general and mining revenues in particular.

In terms of governance in the sector, the foundation of the legal framework has been renewed. The completion of the final implementing regulations should finalize the reform of the regulatory framework. Essential reforms have been completed. The twenty mining agreements signed provide a good set of projects that guarantee exponential development of the mines for at least a decade. However, there is a need to consolidate these reforms and complete some initiatives, particularly those related to economic, social, and environmental impact, as well as monitoring and control of mining activities. All of this will only maintain the momentum if the capacity of the personnel is significantly strengthened as part of the training plan developed, especially in view of the natural turnover of the aging staff. The most significant challenge for governance is the establishment of a system and the necessary resources for effective and ongoing monitoring and control of project implementation in accordance with the Mining Code and agreements within a corruption-free framework. This issue is even more important as the partnership conditions created in the sector, the new projects initiated, could allow for the achievement of essential sector development goals, provided that all stakeholders, especially the State and investors, effectively honor their commitments. Furthermore, it is important to hope that the global market and the economies of partner countries in financing and target markets for the production do not experience crises that affect project development and operations in Guinea. It is also necessary to hope and work towards ensuring that the Covid-19 pandemic is not one of those major crises with medium and long-term effects. The evolution of the global market and the impacts of pandemics are essentially beyond the control of the State, unlike the quality of public policies adopted by the State and the effectiveness of their implementation, which are necessary to maximize the positive impacts of the mines.

The policy of financing local communities with mining revenues is one of the keys to success in maximizing the benefits of mining over the long term. Allocating a portion of mining revenues to these communities is a significant step toward the goal of improving the contribution of mining to Guinea's development. The establishment of the National Fund for Local Development (FNDL) funded by these resources and the Local Economic Development Fund (FODEL) represents a major turning point in this approach. The past decade has been marked by reforms and the effective launch of the investment dynamic in the mines. This strong investment dynamic will gradually slow down as the country moves into the exploitation and transformation of these resources. During this time, the FNDL and FODEL will gain momentum thanks to the revenues generated from these operations. At the current pace, these funds could reach or even exceed 1,200 billion Guinean francs (more than 130 million US dollars) per year by 2030. The importance and regularity of these funds should completely change the territorial aspects of development in the country. Long concentrated in major urban centers, especially the capital city, development efforts now extend to the entire country and are expected to grow over time. These funds will offset the benefits derived solely from the investment process, which will eventually stabilize after the bulk of investments has been realized.

The synergy between mining and other critical sectors for its development is another fundamental aspect of public policies that will be crucial for the future of the mines. The quality of synergy with the energy sector plays a significant role in this agenda. The mining industry has a significant need for energy, especially for local transformation. The solvency of the mining industry itself serves as a lever to facilitate investments in the energy sector. This evident complementarity between the two sectors creates the conditions for synergy, enabling the use of mining to facilitate the financing of energy projects, with a portion dedicated to supporting local transformation. In terms of energy supply, gas and renewable energy sources are natural targets, given the focus on limiting the environmental impacts of mining product transformation. Besides developing partnerships to make gas reliably available at competitive prices, successful gas exploration will boost local processing.

Partnerships should be forged not only within Guinea but also on an international level. Continuing international cooperation will be an asset. Regional energy projects have made significant progress in recent years, particularly within the framework of the organizations for the development of the Gambia River Basin (OMVG) and the Senegal River Basin (OMVS) and the ECOWAS. These projects include the construction of dams and interconnection between countries in the region. One of these projects is the OMVG loop (a 225 kV transmission line) covering 1,677 km to interconnect the national electrical grids of the Gambia, Guinea, Guinea-Bissau, and Senegal. Additionally, there is the CLSG interconnection project (a 225 kV line), spanning 1,349 km, which is part of the West African Power Pool (WAPP) initiative by

ECOWAS. This project, funded by the World Bank, the European Investment Bank, KfW, and the African Development Bank, aims to interconnect Ivory Coast, Liberia, Sierra Leone, and Guinea. In terms of production, the realization of the Sambagalou (128 MW, OMVG) and Koukoutamba (296 MW, OMVS) dams also falls within the framework of this promising sub-regional cooperation. The commissioning of these projects would enable the Guinean mining industry to benefit from surpluses generated by other countries in the sub-region, in addition to its own national production. With a comprehensive national network of transmission lines, all mining areas can be serviced.

In the event of a lack of clear prospects for gas discovery in Guinea in the medium term, another avenue for sub-regional cooperation could be the supply of gas to Senegal, which is close to the north-western region (for bauxite processing), and Côte d'Ivoire, near the south-eastern region (for iron processing). In this case, an evaluation of the feasibility of building gas pipelines between Guinea and these two countries could be considered as part of a mutually beneficial partnership.

Opportunities extend beyond the West African region and involve global energy interconnection that goes beyond Africa. Guinea is at the center of initiatives taken at the continental level and is making efforts to realize African and global cooperation. The creation of the Global Energy Interconnection Development and Cooperation Organization (GEIDCO) in March 2016 is one of these initiatives. This initiative is based, in part, on the assumption of aluminum and steel production in Guinea. The needs of these industries could help justify the construction of high-voltage power lines (up to 1,000 kV) between the Democratic Republic of Congo and Guinea and the utilization of 8 gigawatts of capacity from the Grand Inga hydropower complex at a competitive price.

Cooperation in the field of energy for transformation could also be supplemented or facilitated by inter-state equity participation. This would allow Guinea to position itself well and benefit from the African Continental Free Trade Area (AfCFTA), which came into effect on May 30, 2019.

Another important area of synergy that deserves full attention is the one between mining and agriculture. Mining companies are increasingly investing in the agricultural sector as part of their Corporate Social Responsibility (CSR) initiatives. These actions are complemented by the financing of agricultural activities in the implementation of the National Fund for Local Development (FNDL) and the Economic Local Development Fund (FODEL) by local communities, especially concerning income-generating activities for youth and women. On a larger scale, the growing consideration of agricultural investments combined with mining investments represents a significant advancement in the mines' contribution to the development of the vast employment pool that agriculture represents. This helps offset the relatively low labor intensity in industrial mining activities. A typical example of such an arrangement is the Simandou Blocks 1 and 2 project in which investors commit to creating an agricultural corridor along the *Transguinean* railway with an investment of $150 million. This commitment is in addition to a similar one made for the Boffa-Boké railway corridor currently under construction. The multi-use nature of the infrastructure will accommodate the transportation needs of this future agricultural production and its export, providing even more impact to the investment initiated for mining operations.

The synergy between mining and energy, as well as between mining and agriculture, along with the effective sharing of transportation and evacuation infrastructure, will serve as powerful drivers for economic diversification and the amplification of impacts to the benefit of a significant portion of Guineans. This diversification will be made possible through the positive externalities of mining at the national level and through cooperation with neighboring countries and beyond.

Between 1958 and 2010, the total investments made in the mines were less than $5 billion. From 2011 to 2020, a total investment of $6.4 billion was effectively realized in the sector out of a total commitment of over $25 billion for ongoing projects. This demonstrates the leap that Guinea has made over the past decade. However, with only 25.6% of the committed investments realized, we are still far from the goal. Therefore, we must avoid complacency and maintain strict vigilance during the 2021-2030 decade. The journey is still long, and progress remains fragile. The country is in the midst of a decade-long investment phase in the mines. Only by ensuring the effective realization of planned projects can the sector have a chance to fully play its role in transforming the national economy. Any major disruption at the national or international level can have a destructive effect on these achievements if the sector has not reached a critical point of resilience, preventing it from returning to square one. Resilience is acquired through the consolidation of governance achievements, as well as diversification and local processing of production.

The period from 2010 to 2015 was marked by the launch of reforms. 2015-2020 saw the beginning of the phase of intensive investments. The next decade should first be one of intensified investments and positive impacts (2021-2025), followed by full transformation. Only by achieving these goals can the country reach the point of no return. All eyes and efforts must be focused on reaching this point of no return, which will be another turning point for Guinea: the completion of the foundation for the "post-mining" era, which will involve less dependence on mining in an ever-increasing prosperity.

Conclusion

The Ministry of Mines and Geology is one of the priority economic ministries in Guinea. It is also, along with the Ministries of Territorial Administration, Decentralization, Defense and Security, one of the sectors with the widest active coverage of the territory. The country, which some refuse to call "mining country", relies heavily on mining for the diversification of its economy and its development.

The appointment of a 39-year-old, with no ministerial experience, to lead one of the most important departments surprised many. Since then, more than five years have passed quickly, and much has happened. The relatively long tenure Minister of Mines can naturally be attributed to the trust, support, and understanding of the Head of State toward me. I will always be grateful to him for that.

An explanation for this longevity can also be found in the mindset and attitude I adopted right after my appointment. I made sure not to be consumed by the role immediately after my appointment. From the very next morning, I began to mentally prepare for the inevitable day when I would step down from the position of minister. I tried, always, to stay grounded, remain humble, considering the honor of serving in this role. I adhered to the principle of not doing anything I could not do if I were not a minister, except for some necessary actions related to the exercise of the function itself. I made sure that every day, every hour, I gave my best to serve the country and take actions that would positively impact the lives of my fellow citizens, as if it could all end at any moment. Every day, every hour, I was motivated by the thought of not disappointing the expectations regarding the ministry's mission, those of the young Guineans who deserve to believe in their country, and for whom I needed to contribute to making the appointment of ministers in their thirties normal. Above all, I was driven by the expectations of the population, who are legitimately eager to see more benefits from the mines in their daily lives.

I also chose to serve every moment with dignity, dedication, and loyalty to the mission that was entrusted to me. The only battles I fought, apart from serving, were those aimed at defending my dignity and reputation because I have always believed — and still do — that my best capital was my reputation and relationships.

Taking a step back from the allure and prestige of the position, as well as the daily constraints, allowed me to move forward with greater serenity. There was, however, a lot to contend with, including threats, intimidations, influence peddling, fraudulent actions by some unscrupulous actors, and the constant low blows from those seeking positions or their sponsors, as well as the technical and administrative difficulties specific to mining projects. Surprisingly, these difficulties did not match the social pressure, with its financial implications, surrounding a Minister of Mines, whom everyone believes can solve all their problems, even those beyond the resources and powers of the minister.

Guinea's mines have long been the subject of headlines for scandals and controversies. For almost six years, I decided to fight to refocus the debate on the sector on the essential: mining development. To achieve this, it was necessary to focus on the work, say little and do more, and make no concessions on Guinea's fundamental interests. It also meant staying away from certain social events and extravagances. It was a delicate balancing act to remain discreet in such an exposed position, carefully choosing media appearances, being seen only where one must be seen, and communicating only about the substance of actions and results.

It was necessary to defend and protect the investment (not to be confused with the investor) made in accordance with the laws, for the benefit of all, even at the risk of being misunderstood at times. There were obstacles, but we could only overcome them by establishing strong partnerships with ministry colleagues, other government officials, investors, local authorities, technical and financial partners, local elected officials, the National Assembly, and more. In five years, we successfully have over twenty agreements adopted by all parties at the National Assembly. This achievement was largely due to the strong involvement of the parliamentary committee responsible for mining and the focus of MPs from all parties on the interests of the country and that of the affected regions.

Despite the significant progress made, not everything was perfect, complete, or even initiated in some cases. Not everything could be accomplished not only because the task was vast, but also because each period has its own priorities, contingencies, and constraints. It is about making the best use of the situation for Guinea, taking risks at times to obtain more for the country, with conviction, while considering these constraints. Negotiations, strategic choices, and conflict management posture have followed this rule. What we can do today, we might not have been able to do when we did not have a strong position in the market for raw products. What we will be able to do tomorrow, in a mature position, we cannot do today. This can be true for transformation, revenues, local content, and more.

What we accomplished must be consolidated and, of course, improved to stay on course. To achieve this, it will certainly require that our successors, as the popular saying goes, do not throw the baby out with the bathwater. Just as we ourselves have made sure not to commit this endemic mistake in Guinea. To achieve this, it will certainly be necessary to deepen the internal reforms that have been initiated, allocate the necessary resources, strengthen the culture of merit, accountability, and transparency, as well as government solidarity around mining projects.

Everything has been done in recent years to make the mining industry take off. There has been no luck, and there will not be any. The results today and the encouraging prospects are the result of tireless efforts by the stakeholders, even though many, perhaps out of impatience, do not yet realize the progress made in the country's mines.

Development is a long process. This is even more true for the development of the mining sector. It requires commitment and rigor to achieve it. It requires perseverance, despite impatience. It requires passion, constantly. After more than five years of passionate commitment and perseverance for success, I made my modest contribution to the development of the sector. Despite obstacles and challenges, I was determined to lay strong foundations for the irreversible development of Guinean mines. I made the most of every minute I spent leading the ministry, taking pleasure in contributing to the construction of this edifice. I did my best and achieved some results, as a citizen always aspiring to more and better for his country. It was a school. It was dense. It was difficult at times. It was, for sure, imperfect, like any human work. But how rich and exhilarating it was!

Structures éditoriales du groupe L'Harmattan

L'Harmattan Italie
Via degli Artisti, 15
10124 Torino
harmattan.italia@gmail.com

L'Harmattan Hongrie
Kossuth l. u. 14-16.
1053 Budapest
harmattan@harmattan.hu

L'Harmattan Sénégal
10 VDN en face Mermoz
BP 45034 Dakar-Fann
senharmattan@gmail.com

L'Harmattan Cameroun
TSINGA/FECAFOOT
BP 11486 Yaoundé
inkoukam@gmail.com

L'Harmattan Burkina Faso
Achille Somé – tengnule@hotmail.fr

L'Harmattan Guinée
Almamya, rue KA 028 OKB Agency
BP 3470 Conakry
harmattanguinee@yahoo.fr

L'Harmattan RDC
185, avenue Nyangwe
Commune de Lingwala – Kinshasa
matangilamusadila@yahoo.fr

L'Harmattan Congo
67, boulevard Denis-Sassou-N'Guesso
BP 2874 Brazzaville
harmattan.congo@yahoo.fr

L'Harmattan Mali
Sirakoro-Meguetana V31
Bamako
syllaka@yahoo.fr

L'Harmattan Togo
Djidjole – Lomé
Maison Amela
face EPP BATOME
ddamela@aol.com

L'Harmattan Côte d'Ivoire
Résidence Karl – Cité des Arts
Abidjan-Cocody
03 BP 1588 Abidjan
espace_harmattan.ci@hotmail.fr

L'Harmattan Algérie
22, rue Moulay-Mohamed
31000 Oran
info2@harmattan-algerie.com

L'Harmattan Maroc
5, rue Ferrane-Kouicha, Talaâ-Elkbira
Chrableyine, Fès-Médine
30000 Fès
harmattan.maroc@gmail.com

Nos librairies en France

Librairie internationale
16, rue des Écoles – 75005 Paris
librairie.internationale@harmattan.fr
01 40 46 79 11
www.librairieharmattan.com

Librairie l'Espace Harmattan
21 bis, rue des Écoles – 75005 paris
librairie.espace@harmattan.fr
01 43 29 49 42

Lib. sciences humaines & histoire
21, rue des Écoles – 75005 paris
librairie.sh@harmattan.fr
01 46 34 13 71
www.librairieharmattansh.com

Lib. Méditerranée & Moyen-Orient
7, rue des Carmes – 75005 Paris
librairie.mediterranee@harmattan.fr
01 43 29 71 15

Librairie Le Lucernaire
53, rue Notre-Dame-des-Champs – 75006 Paris
librairie@lucernaire.fr
01 42 22 67 13